Best Ever
Knock Knock Jokes

MARKS &
SPENCER

Marks and Spencer p.l.c.
Baker Street, London W1U 8EP
www.marksandspencer.com

Copyright©Exclusive Editions 2001

This book was created by Magpie Books,
an imprint of Constable & Robinson Ltd

ISBN 1-84273-168-8

A copy of the British Library Cataloguing-in-Publication Data
is available from the British Library

Contents

Chapter 1

Girls' names

ANNA

Knock knock.
Who's there?
Anna.
Anna who?
Annamazingly good joke.

Knock knock.
Who's there?
Abby.
Abby who?
Abby go lucky.

Knock knock.
Who's there?
Ada.
Ada who?
Ada lot for breakfast.

Knock knock.
Who's there?
Adelaide.
Adelaide who?
Adelaide an egg, you'd have been surprised!

Knock knock.
Who's there?
Agatha.
Agatha who?
Agatha you're not very fond of me.

Knock knock.
Who's there?
Aida.
Aida who?
Aida whole box of chocolates and I feel really sick.

Knock knock.
Who's there?
Aileen.
Aileen who?
Aileen against my Rolls Royce.

Knock knock.
Who's there?
Aleta.
Aleta who?
Aleta from your bank manager.

Knock knock.
Who's there?
Ali.
Ali who?
Ali cat.

Knock knock.
Who's there?
Alice.
Alice who?
Alice on your new house.

Knock knock.
Who's there?
Alison.
Alison who?
Alison wonderland.

Knock knock.
Who's there?
Alma.
Alma who?
Almany times do I have to knock?

Knock knock.
Who's there?
Alma.
Alma who?
Alma lovin'.

Knock knock.
Who's there?
Andrea.
Andrea who?
Andrea of the house is another door.

Knock knock.
Who's there?
Anita.
Anita who?
Anita way of putting it.

Knock knock.
Who's there?
Althea.
Althea who?
Althea in court.

Knock knock.
Who's there?
Amanda.
Amanda who?
Amanda the table.

Knock knock.
Who's there?
Amber.
Amber who?
Amberter than I was yesterday.

Knock knock.
Who's there?
Amber.
Amber who?
Ambersting to go
   to the bathroom.

Knock knock.
Who's there?
Amy.
Amy who?
Amy for the top.

Knock knock.
Who's there?
Anaïs.
Anaïs who?
Anaïs cup of tea, please.

Knock knock.
Who's there?
Anna.
Anna who?
Annamazingly good joke.

Knock knock.
Who's there?
Annabel.
Annabel who?
Annabel would be useful on this door.

Knock knock.
Who's there?
Annette.
Annette who?
Annette curtain looks
  good in the window.

Knock knock.
Who's there?
Annie.
Annie who?
Annie one you like.

Knock knock.
Who's there?
Anya.
Anya who?
Anya best behaviour.

Knock knock.
Who's there?
April.
April who?
April will make you feel better.

Knock knock.
Who's there?
Audrey.
Audrey who?
Audrey to pay for this?

Knock knock.
Who's there?
Audrey.
Audrey who?
Audrey another drink.

Knock knock.
Who's there?
Augusta.
Augusta who?
Augusta wind will blow the witch away.

Knock knock.
Who's there?
Aurora.
Aurora who?
Aurora's just come from a big lion!

Knock knock.
Who's there?
Ava.
Ava who?
Ava good mind to leave you.

Knock knock.
Who's there?
Avis.
Avis who?
Avisibly shaken person.

Knock knock.
Who's there?
Avril.
Avril who?
Avril flowers instead of artificial.

Knock knock.
Who's there?
Barbara.
Barbara who?
(*sing*) "Barbara black sheep, have you any wool?"

Knock knock.
Who's there?
Barbie.
Barbie who?
Barbie Q.

Knock knock.
Who's there?
Bea.
Bea who?
Bea love and open the door.

Knock knock.
Who's there?
Bella.
Bella who?
Bella the ball.

Knock knock.
Who's there?
Belle.
Belle who?
Belle-t up and open the door.

Knock knock.
Who's there?
Belle.
Belle who?
Belle bottom trousers are back in fashion.

Knock knock.
Who's there?
Bernadette.
Bernadette who?
Bernadette my dinner.

Knock knock.
Who's there?
Bertha.
Bertha who?
Bertha day girl.

Knock knock.
Who's there?
Bertha.
Bertha who?
Bertha boat in a dry dock.

Knock knock.
Who's there?
Beryl.
Beryl who?
Berylliant idea.

Knock knock.
Who's there?
Beth.
Beth who?
Beth foot forward.

Knock knock.
Who's there?
Beth.
Beth who?
Bether late than never.

Knock knock.
Who's there?
Bethany.
Bethany who?
Bethany good shows recently?

Knock knock.
Who's there?
Bette.
Bette who?
Bette of roses.

Knock knock.
Who's there?
Bettina.
Bettina who?
Bettina minute you'll
  go to sleep.

Knock knock.
Who's there?
Betty.
Betty who?
Betty earns a lot of money.

Knock knock.
Who's there?
Bianca.
Bianca who?
Biancared safely – there's a storm brewing.

Knock knock.
Who's there?
Bridget.
Bridget who?
Bridget on the River Kwai.

Knock knock.
Who's there?
Bridie.
Bridie who?
Bridie light of the silvery moon.

Knock knock.
Who's there?
Bronwen.
Bronwen who?
Bronwen you return from your holiday.

Knock knock.
Who's there?
Caitlin.
Caitlin who?
Caitlin you my dress
tonight – I'm wearing it.

Knock knock.
Who's there?
Camilla.
Camilla who?
Camilla minute!

Knock knock.
Who's there?
Candice.
Candice who?
Candice be love?

Knock knock.
Who's there?
Candida.
Candida who?
Candida's capital is Ottawa.

Knock knock.
Who's there?
Candy.
Candy who?
Candy pend on me.

Knock knock.
Who's there?
Carlene.
Carlene who?
Carlene against that wall!

Knock knock.
Who's there?
Carlotta.
Carlotta who?
Carlotta use with no wheels.

Knock knock.
Who's there?
Carmel.
Carmel who?
Carmelted down for scrap.

Knock knock.
Who's there?
Carmen.
Carmen who?
Carmen like best is a Ferrari.

Knock knock.
Who's there?
Carol.
Carol who?
Carol go if you switch the
ignition on.

Knock knock.
Who's there?
Carolyn.
Carolyn who?
Carolyn of rope with you.

Knock knock.
　Who's there?
　　Carrie.
　　Carrie who?
　　Carrie on with what
　　you are doing.

Knock knock.
　Who's there?
Carrie.
Carrie who?
Carrie your bags mister.

Knock knock.
Who's there?
Cassie.
Cassie who?
Cassie you some time?

Knock knock.
Who's there?
Cecile.
Cecile who?
Cecile th-the w-windows. Th-there's
　a m-monster out there.

Knock knock.
Who's there?
Cecily.
Cecily who?
Cecily is an island in the Mediterranean.

Knock knock.
Who's there?
Celeste.
Celeste who?
Celeste time I come calling.

Knock knock.
Who's there?
Cindy.
Cindy who?
Cindy parcel, special delivery.

Knock knock.
Who's there?
Clara.
Clara who?
Clara space on the table.

Knock knock.
Who's there?
Claudette.
Claudette who?
Claudette a whole cake.

Knock knock.
Who's there?
Claudia.
Claudia who?
Claudia eyes out, didn't I?

Knock knock.
Who's there?
Colleen.
Colleen who?
Colleen yourself up,
  you're a mess!

Knock knock.
Who's there?
Corrinne.
Corrinne who?
Corrine the bell now.

Knock knock.
Who's there?
Courtney.
Courtney who?
Courtney robbers lately?

Knock knock.
Who's there?
Cynthia.
Cynthia who?
Cynthia won't listen, I'll keep shouting.

Knock knock.
Who's there?
Daisy.
Daisy who?
Daisy that you are in,
   but I don't believe them.

Knock knock.
Who's there?
Dana.
Dana who?
Dana you mind.

Knock knock.
Who's there?
Danielle.
Danielle who?
Danielle so loud, I heard you the first time.

Knock knock.
Who's there?
Dawn.
Dawn who?
Dawn *do* anything I wouldn't do.

Knock knock.
Who's there?
Debbie.
Debbie who?
Debbie or not Debbie, that
  is the question.

Knock knock.
Who's there?
Deirdre.
Deirdre who?
Deirdreams or nightmares?

Knock knock.
Who's there?
Delia.
Delia who?
Delia cards on the table.

Knock knock.
Who's there?
Della.
Della who?
Della tell ya that I love ya?

Knock knock.
Who's there?
Delphine.
Delphine who?
Delphine fine, thanks.

Knock knock.
Who's there?
Denise.
Denise who?
Denise are above de feet.

Knock knock.
Who's there?
Diana.
Diana who?
Diana thirst – a glass of water, please.

Knock knock.
Who's there?
Dilys.
Dilys who?
Dilysious food.

Knock knock.
Who's there?
Dionne.
Dionne who?
Dionne my last exam.

Knock knock.
Who's there?
Dolly.
Dolly who?
Dolly't them in, they're dangerous.

Knock knock.
Who's there?
Donna.
Donna who?
Donna you know? Isa Luigi.

Knock knock.
Who's there?
Dora.
Dora who?
Dora steel.

Knock knock.
Who's there?
Dora.
Dora who?
Dora funny face on the blackboard.

Knock knock.
Who's there?
Doris.
Doris who?
Dorisk a cream cake
– it won't hurt you.

Knock knock.
Who's there?
Dorothy.
Dorothy who?
(sing) "Dorothynk I'm sexy?"

Knock knock.
Who's there?
Dot.
Dot who?
Dotty about you.

Knock knock.
Who's there?
Edie.
Edie who?
Edie come, edie go.

Knock knock.
Who's there?
Edna.
Edna who?
Edna clouds.

Knock knock.
Who's there?
Effa.
Effa who?
Effa boy!

Knock knock.
Who's there?
Effie.
Effie who?
Effie'd known you were coming,
  he'd have stayed home.

Knock knock.
Who's there?
Eileen.
Eileen who?
Eileen against the door.

Knock knock.
Who's there?
Elizabeth.
Elizabeth who?
Elizabeth of knowledge is a dangerous thing.

Knock knock.
Who's there?
Ella.
Ella who?
Ella've good night!

Knock knock.
Who's there?
Ellen.
Ellen who?
Ellen high water.

Knock knock.
Who's there?
Miss Ellie.
Miss Ellie who?
Miss Ellie good shows lately?

Knock knock.
Who's there?
Ellie.
Ellie who?
Elliecopters take off vertically.

Knock knock.
Who's there?
Elly.
Elly who?
Ellymentary, my dear Watson.

Knock knock.
Who's there?
Elsie.
Elsie who?
Elsie you in court!

Knock knock.
Who's there?
Emma.
Emma who?
Emma new neighbour – come round for tea.

Knock knock.
Who's there?
Enid.
Enid who?
Enid a glass of water.

Knock knock.
Who's there?
Erica.
Erica who?
Erica'd the last sweet.

Knock knock.
Who's there?
Erin.
Erin who?
Erin your lungs.

Knock knock.
Who's there?
Esme.
Esme who?
Esme, only me.

Knock knock.
Who's there?
Eunice.
Eunice who?
Eunice is like your nephew.

Knock knock.
Who's there?
Eva.
Eva who?
Eva had a smack in the mouth?

Knock knock.
Who's there?
Eve.
Eve who?
Eve-ho, here we go.

Knock knock.
Who's there?
Evie.
Evie who?
Evie weather today, isn't it?

Knock knock.
Who's there?
Fanny.
Fanny who?
Fanny you not knowing who I am!

Knock knock.
Who's there?
Faye.
Faye who?
Fayeding away.

Knock knock.
Who's there?
Felicity.
Felicity who?
Felicity is getting more polluted every day.

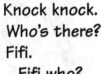

Knock knock.
Who's there?
Fifi.
Fifi who?
Fifiling c-cold, p-please l-let m-me in.

Knock knock.
Who's there?
Fiona.
Fiona who?
Fiona large house and a car.

Knock knock.
Who's there?
Fleur.
Fleur who?
Fleuride toothpaste.

Knock knock.
Who's there?
Flo.
Flo who?
Flo your candles out.

Knock knock.
Who's there?
Flora.
Flora who?
Florat the top of the block.

Knock knock.
Who's there?
Flossie.
Flossie who?
Flossie your teeth every day.

Knock knock.
Who's there?
Frances.
Frances who?
Frances on the other side of the English Channel.

Knock knock.
Who's there?
Françoise.
Françoise who?
Françoise once a great empire.

Knock knock.
Who's there?
Freda.
Freda who?
Freda from prison – she was innocent.

Knock knock.
Who's there?
Gail.
Gail who?
Gail of laughter.

Knock knock.
Who's there?
Gail.
Gail who?
Gail warning to shipping.

Knock knock.
Who's there?
Germaine.
Germaine who?
Germaine you don't recognise me?

Knock knock.
Who's there?
Gertie.
Gertie who?
Gertiesy call!

Knock knock.
Who's there?
Gilda.
Gilda who?
Gilda the picture frame.

Knock knock.
Who's there?
Gill.
Gill who?
Gill-ted lover seeking revenge.

Knock knock.
Who's there?
Giselle.
Giselle who?
Gisellegant and very pretty.

Knock knock.
Who's there?
Gita.
Gita who?
Gita job!

Knock knock.
Who's there?
Gladys.
Gladys who?
Gladys letter isn't a bill.

Knock knock.
Who's there?
Grace.
Grace who?
Grace skies are over us.

Knock knock.
Who's there?
Grace.
Grace who?
Graced my knee.

Knock knock.
Who's there?
Greta.
Greta who?
Greta job at the railway station.

Knock knock.
Who's there?
Guinevere.
Guinevere who?
Guinevere going to get together?

Knock knock.
Who's there?
Hannah.
Hannah who?
Hannah cloth out to dry.

Knock knock.
Who's there?
Harriet.
Harriet who?
Harriet up!

Knock knock.
Who's there?
Hattie.
Hattie who?
Hattie known, he wouldn't have done it.

Knock knock.
Who's there?
Hazel.
Hazel who?
Hazel restrict your vision.

Knock knock.
Who's there?
Heather.
Heather who?
Heather pothtman come yet?

Knock knock.
Who's there?
Hedda.
Hedda who?
Hedda ball in the goal.

Knock knock.
Who's there?
Heidi.
Heidi who?
Heidi Clare war on you.

Knock knock.
Who's there?
Helga.
Helga who?
Helgard her with his life.

Knock knock.
Who's there?
Hester.
Hester who?
Hester la vista baby!

Knock knock.
Who's there?
Hilda.
Hilda who?
Hilda'mand to know your name.

Knock knock.
Who's there?
Holly.
Holly who?
Hollylujah!

Knock knock.
Who's there?
Honor Claire.
Honor Claire who?
Honor Claire day, you can
 see for miles.

Knock knock.
Who's there?
Hope.
Hope who?
Hope you'll have me.

Knock knock.
Who's there?
Ida.
Ida who?
Ida bought a different knocker if I'd been you.

Knock knock.
Who's there?
Ida.
Ida who?
Ida know.

Knock knock.
Who's there?
Imogen.
Imogen who?
Imogenuine person.

Knock knock.
Who's there?
Ina.
Ina who?
Ina minute!

Knock knock.
Who's there?
Ina Claire.
Ina Claire who?
Ina Claire day you can see France.

Knock knock.
Who's there?
Ina Minnie.
Ina Minnie who?
Ina Minnie miney mo.

Knock knock.
Who's there?
India.
India who?
India there's a bag belonging to me.

Knock knock.
Who's there?
Ines.
Ines who?
Inespecial place I'll hide your present.

Knock knock.
Who's there?
Ingrid.
Ingrid who?
Ingrid sorrow I have to leave you.

Knock knock.
Who's there?
Iona.
Iona who?
Iona house of my own, you know.

Knock knock.
Who's there?
Ira.
Ira who?
Ira car and drive yourself.

Knock knock.
Who's there?
Iris.
Iris who?
Iris you would open the door.

Knock knock.
Who's there?
Iris.
Iris who?
Iris stew and dumplings.

Knock knock.
Who's there?
Isabel.
Isabel who?
Isabel necessary
  on a bicycle?

Knock knock.
Who's there?
Isadore.
Isadore who?
Isadore on the right way round?

Knock knock.
Who's there?
Isla.
Isla who?
Isla be seeing you!

Knock knock.
Who's there?
Ivana.
Ivana who?
Ivana be alone.

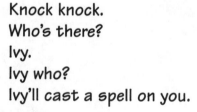

Knock knock.
Who's there?
Ivy.
Ivy who?
Ivy'll cast a spell on you.

Knock knock.
Who's there?
Jackie.
Jackie who?
Jackie'n that job – it's killing you.

Knock knock.
Who's there?
Jacqueline.
Jacqueline who?
Jacqueline Hyde.

Knock knock.
Who's there?
Jade.
Jade who?
Jade a whole pie today.

Knock knock.
Who's there?
Jan.
Jan who?
Jan and bread.

Knock knock.
Who's there?
Janet.
Janet who?
Janet a big fish?

Knock knock.
Who's there?
Janet.
Janet who?
Janetors are the
  same as caretakers.

Knock knock.
Who's there?
Jasmine.
Jasmine who?
Jasmine like to play in jazz bands.

Knock knock.
Who's there?
Jean.
Jean who?
Jeanius – you just don't recognise it.

Knock knock.
Who's there?
Jeanette.
Jeanette who?
Jeanette has too many holes in it, the fish will escape.

Knock knock.
Who's there?
Jenny.
Jenny who?
Jenny-d anything from the shops?

Knock knock.
Who's there?
Jess.
Jess who?
Jess l'il ol' me.

Knock knock.
Who's there?
Jess.
Jess who?
Jessture of good will.

Knock knock.
Who's there?
Jessica.
Jessica who?
Jessica lot up last night?

Knock knock.
Who's there?
Joan.
Joan who?
Joan call us, we'll call you.

Knock knock.
Who's there?
Joan.
Joan who?
Joan you know your own daughter?

Knock knock.
Who's there?
Joanna.
Joanna who?
Joanna smack? Just let
  me in.

Knock knock.
Who's there?
Jocelyn.
Jocelyn who?
Jocelyn for the best position.

Knock knock.
Who's there?
Joy.
Joy who?
Joyl your bike regularly?

Knock knock.
Who's there?
Juanita.
Juanita who?
Juanita big meal?

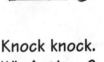

Knock knock.
Who's there?
Judith.
Judith who?
Judither about like this all the time?

Knock knock.
Who's there?
Judy.
Judy who?
Judy liver newspapers still?

Knock knock.
Who's there?
Julia.
Julia who?
Julia at all the guys like that?

Knock knock.
Who's there?
Julie.
Julie who?
Julie'n on this door a lot?

Knock knock.
Who's there?
Julie.
Julie who?
Juliek official secrets?

Knock knock.
Who's there?
Juliet.
Juliet who?
Juliet him get away with that?

Knock knock.
Who's there?
June.
June who?
June know how to open a door?

Knock knock.
Who's there?
Juno.
Juno who?
Juno how to get out of here?

Knock knock.
Who's there?
Justine.
Justine who?
Justine the nick of time.

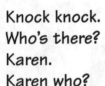

Knock knock.
Who's there?
Karen.
Karen who?
Karen this for me – it's heavy.

Knock knock.
Who's there?
Katherine.
Katherine who?
Katherine together for a social evening.

Knock knock.
Who's there?
Kathy.
Kathy who?
Kathy you again?

Knock knock.
Who's there?
Kay.
Kay who?
Kayvewomen like cavemen.

Knock knock.
Who's there?
Kiki.
Kiki who?
Kiki's stuck in the l-lock – let me in.

Knock knock.
Who's there?
Kim.
Kim who?
Kim too late.

Knock knock.
Who's there?
Kristin.
Kristin who?
Kristining robe.

Knock knock.
Who's there?
Lacey.
Lacey who?
Lacey crazy days.

Knock knock.
Who's there?
Lana.
Lana who?
Lana the free.

Knock knock.
Who's there?
Leah.
Leah who?
Leahn egg for my tea.

Knock knock.
Who's there?
Leigh.
Leigh who?
Leigh've it to me.

Knock knock.
Who's there?
Leonie.
Leonie who.
Leonie one I love.

Knock knock.
Who's there?
Leslie.
Leslie who?
Leslie've town now before they catch us.

Knock knock.
Who's there?
Lily.
Lily who?
Lily livered varmint!

Knock knock.
Who's there?
Liz.
Liz who?
Liz see what you look like.

Knock knock.
Who's there?
Liz.
Liz who?
Lizen carefully, I will say this only once.

Knock knock.
Who's there?
Lois.
Lois who?
Loist of the low.

Knock knock.
Who's there?
Lorraine.
Lorraine who?
Lorraine in Spain falls mainly on the plain.

Knock knock.
Who's there?
Lotte.
Lotte who?
Lotte sense.

Knock knock.
Who's there?
Louise.
Louise who?
Louise coming to tea today.

Knock knock.
Who's there?
Lucetta.
Lucetta who?
Lucetta a difficult problem.

Knock knock.
Who's there?
Lucille.
Lucille who?
Lucille-ing is dangerous to live under.

Knock knock.
Who's there?
Lucinda.
Lucinda who?
(*sing*) "Lucinda sky with diamonds ..."

Knock knock.
Who's there?
Lucy.
Lucy who?
Lucylastic can let you down.

Knock knock.
Who's there?
Lydia.
Lydia who?
Lydia teapot's cracked.

Knock knock.
Who's there?
Lyn.
Lyn who?
Lynger a little longer.

Knock knock.
Who's there?
Madeline.
Madeline who?
Madeline with my affairs.

Knock knock.
Who's there?
Mae.
Mae who?
(*sing*) "Mae be it's because I'm a Londoner."

Knock knock.
Who's there?
Mai.
Mai who?
Mai animals are like children to me.

Knock knock.
Who's there?
Mamie.
Mamie who?
Mamie a new dress.

Knock knock.
Who's there?
Mandy.
Mandy who?
Mandy guns, the enemy is coming.

Knock knock.
Who's there?
Marcia.
Marcia who?
Marcia me!

Knock knock.
Who's there?
Margie.
Margie who?
Margie-rine or butter on your toast?

Knock knock.
Who's there?
Margo.
Margo who?
Margo, you're not needed now.

Knock knock.
Who's there?
Maria.
Maria who?
Marial name is Mary.

Knock knock.
Who's there?
Maria.
Maria who?
Maria window is all steamed up.

Knock knock.
Who's there?
Marian.
Marian who?
Mariand her little lamb.

Knock knock.
Who's there?
Marie.
Marie who?
Marieson for knocking is to be let in.

Knock knock.
Who's there?
Marie.
Marie who?
Marie for love.

Knock knock.
Who's there?
Marietta.
Marietta who?
Marietta whole loaf!

Knock knock.
Who's there?
Marigold.
Marigold who?
Marigold and be rich.

Knock knock.
Who's there?
Marilyn.
Marilyn who?
Marilyn, she'll make you a good wife.

Knock knock.
Who's there?
Marion.
Marion who?
Marion idiot and repent at leisure.

Knock knock.
Who's there?
Marsha.
Marsha who?
Marshans have landed.

Knock knock.
Who's there?
Martha.
Martha who?
Martha boys next door are hurting me!

Knock knock.
Who's there?
Mary.
Mary who?
That's what I keep wondering.

Knock knock.
Who's there?
Maud.
Maud who?
Maudrama by the garden gate.

Knock knock.
Who's there?
Maude.
Maude who?
Mauden my job's worth.

Knock knock.
Who's there?
Maude.
Maude who?
Mauden living.

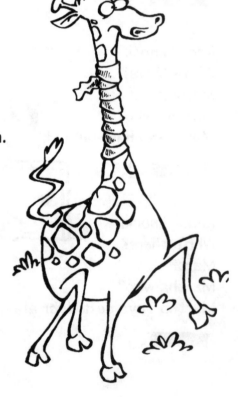

Knock knock.
Who's there?
Mavis.
Mavis who?
Mavis be the best day of your life.

Knock knock.
Who's there?
Maxine.
Maxine who?
Maxine a lot of things.

Knock knock.
Who's there?
May.
May who?
Maybe it's a friend at the door.

Knock knock.
Who's there?
Maya.
Maya who?
Maya turn up unexpectedly?

Knock knock.
Who's there?
Meg.
Meg who?
Meg a fuss.

Knock knock.
Who's there?
Megan.
Megan who?
Megan a loud noise.

Knock knock.
Who's there?
Melinda.
Melinda who?
Melinda fiver? I'll never get it back.

Knock knock.
Who's there?
Michelle.
Michelle who?
Michelle has the sounds of the sea in it.

Knock knock.
Who's there?
Milly.
Milly who?
Milly-ons of men can't be wrong.

Knock knock.
Who's there?
Mimi.
Mimi who?
Mimi b-bicycle's b-broken.

Knock knock.
Who's there?
Minnie.
Minnie who?
Minnie people want to come in.

Knock knock.
Who's there?
Minnie.
Minnie who?
Minniestrone soup, please.

Knock knock.
Who's there?
Miranda.
Miranda who?
Miranda friend want to come in.

Knock knock.
Who's there?
Moira.
Moira who?
Moira fool than a knave.

Knock knock.
Who's there?
Moira.
Moira who?
Moiracles do happen.

Knock knock.
Who's there?
Mona.
Mona who?
Mona lawn for three pounds.

Knock knock.
Who's there?
Morag.
Morag who?
Moraggro from you and I'll get really angry.

Knock knock.
Who's there.
Nadia.
Nadia who?
Nadia head if you want me to come in.

Knock knock.
Who's there?
Nancy.
Nancy who?
Nancy a piece of cake?

Knock knock.
Who's there?
Nell.
Nell who?
Nell is where bad people go.

Knock knock.
Who's there?
Nell.
Nell who?
Nelly the elephant.

Knock knock.
Who's there?
Nelly.
Nelly who?
Nelly midnight, Cinderella!

Knock knock.
Who's there?
Nicky.
Nicky who?
Nicky nacks.

Knock knock.
Who's there?
Nicolette.
Nicolette who?
Nicolette and steam it open.

Knock knock.
Who's there?
Nola.
Nola who?
Nolaner driver may drive a car alone.

Knock knock.
Who's there?
Norma.
Norma who?
Normally the butler opens the door.

Knock knock.
Who's there?
Odette.
Odette who?
Odette I can't repay.

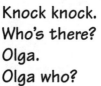

Knock knock.
Who's there?
Olga.
Olga who?
Olga home now.

Knock knock.
Who's there?
Olive.
Olive who?
Olive in this house – what are you doing there?

Knock knock.
Who's there?
Olive.
Olive who?
Olive to regret it.

Knock knock.
Who's there?
Olivia.
Olivia who?
Olivia'l is great for cooking.

Knock knock.
Who's there?
Onya.
Onya who?
Onya marks, get set, go.

Knock knock.
Who's there?
Pam.
Pam who?
Pamper yourself.

Knock knock.
Who's there?
Pammy.
Pammy who?
Pammy something nice when you are at the shops!

Knock knock.
Who's there?
Patty.
Patty who?
Patty-cake.

Knock knock.
Who's there?
Pearl.
Pearl who?
Pearl like a happy cat.

Knock knock.
Who's there?
Peg.
Peg who?
Peg your pardon, I've got the wrong door.

Knock knock.
Who's there?
Penny.
Penny who?
Penny for your thoughts.

Knock knock.
Who's there?
Petal.
Petal who?
Petal fast, we're nearly there.

Knock knock.
Who's there?
Petula.
Petula who?
Petulaugh at all these jokes.

Knock knock.
Who's there?
Philippa.
Philippa who?
Philippa bath – I'm really dirty.

Knock knock.
Who's there?
Phoebe.
Phoebe who?
Phoebe way above my price.

Knock knock.
Who's there?
Phyllis.
Phyllis who?
Phyllis up.

Knock knock.
Who's there?
Polly.
Polly who?
Polly other one, it's got bells on.

Knock knock.
Who's there?
Poppy.
Poppy who?
Poppy'n any time you like.

Knock knock.
Who's there?
Portia.
Portia who?
Portia the door – it's stuck.

Knock knock.
Who's there?
Posie.
Posie who?
Posie hard questions.

Knock knock.
Who's there?
Prue.
Prue who?
Prue'f of the pudding is in the eating.

Knock knock.
Who's there?
Rena.
Rena who?
Renamok in the shopping centre.

Knock knock.
Who's there?
Renata.
Renata who?
Renata sugar. Can I borrow some?

Knock knock.
Who's there?
Rhoda.
Rhoda who?
Rhoda horse around Hyde Park.

Knock knock.
Who's there?
Rhona.
Rhona who?
Rhonaround town.

Knock knock.
Who's there?
Rhonda.
Rhonda who?
Rhonda why?

Knock knock.
Who's there?
Rita.
Rita who?
Rita novel.

Knock knock.
Who's there?
Rosalie.
Rosalie who?
Rosalie and went to bed late.

Knock knock.
Who's there?
Rose.
Rose who?
Rose early one morning.

Knock knock.
Who's there?
Rosemary.
Rosemary who?
Rosemary after a good night's sleep.

Knock knock.
Who's there?
Rosina.
Rosina who?
Rosina vase.

Knock knock.
Who's there?
Roxie.
Roxie who?
Roxie Horror Show.

Knock knock.
Who's there?
Ruth.
Ruth who?
Ruthless people.

Knock knock.
Who's there?
Sacha.
Sacha who?
Sacha money in the bank?

Knock knock.
Who's there?
Saffron.
Saffron who?
Saffron a chair and it collapsed.

Knock knock.
Who's there?
Sal.
Sal who?
Salarming news, isn't it?

Knock knock.
Who's there?
Sally.
Sally who?
Sally everything you've got.

Knock knock.
Who's there?
Sally.
Sally who?
Sallygators I'm afraid of!

Knock knock.
Who's there?
Samantha.
Samantha who?
Samantha baby have gone for a walk.

Knock knock.
Who's there?
Sandra.
Sandra who?
Sandrabout your toes on the beach.

Knock knock.
Who's there?
Sandy.
Sandy who?
Sandy shore.

Knock knock.
Who's there?
Sarah.
Sarah who?
Sarah doctor in the house?

Knock knock.
Who's there?
Selina.
Selina who?
Selina meat is better for you.

Knock knock.
Who's there?
Serena.
Serena who?
Serena round the corner.

Knock knock.
Who's there?
Sharon.
Sharon who?
Sharon share alike — would you
  like some of my chocolate?

Knock knock.
Who's there?
Shelby.
Shelby who?
(*sing*) "Shelby coming round the mountain
  when she comes."

Knock knock.
Who's there?
Sheena.
Sheena who?
Sheena pair of socks lying around?

Knock knock.
Who's there?
Sherry.
Sherry who?
Sherry trifle!

Knock knock.
Who's there?
Shirley.
Shirley who?
Shirley you know who I am!

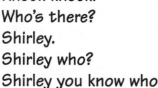

Knock knock.
Who's there?
Sigrid.
Sigrid who?
Sigrid Service – open up!

Knock knock.
Who's there?
Sonia.
Sonia who?
Sonia shoe – it's stinking the house out.

Knock knock.
Who's there?
Sophia.
Sophia who?
Sophia nothing – there's nothing to be afraid of!

Knock knock.
Who's there?
Sorrel.
Sorrel who?
Sorrel about the mess.

Knock knock.
Who's there?
Stacey.
Stacey who?
Stacey what happens next.

Knock knock.
Who's there?
Stella.
Stella who?
Stella lot from
the rich people.

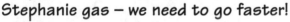

Knock knock.
Who's there?
Stephanie.
Stephanie who?
Stephanie gas – we need to go faster!

Knock knock.
Who's there?
Sue.
Sue who?
Sue'n you will know.

Knock knock.
Who's there?
Sybil.
Sybil who?
Sybiling rivalry.

Knock knock.
Who's there?
Tamsin.
Tamsin who?
Tamsin time again I come to the wrong house.

Knock knock.
Who's there?
Tania.
Tania who?
Tania self round, you'll see.

Knock knock.
Who's there?
Tara.
Tara who?
Tararaboomdeay.

Knock knock.
Who's there?
Tess.
Tess who?
Tess a coin to decide.

Knock knock.
Who's there?
Thea.
Thea who?
Thea later, alligator.

Knock knock.
Who's there?
Theresa.
Theresa who?
Theresa green.

Knock knock.
Who's there?
Thisbe.
Thisbe who?
Thisbeef is too tough.

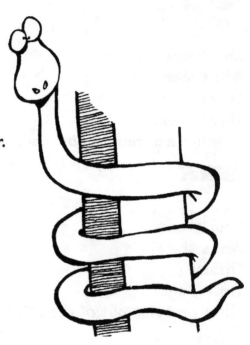

Knock knock.
Who's there?
Thomasina.
Thomasina who?
Thomasina ghost by the looks of him.

Knock knock.
Who's there?
Thora.
Thora who?
Thoran ice cube with some hot water.

Knock knock.
Who's there?
Tiffany.
Tiffany who?
Tiffany rubbish out of the bag before you use it.

Knock knock.
Who's there?
Tilly.
Tilly who?
Tilly cows come home.

Knock knock.
Who's there?
Tina.
Tina who?
Tina tomatoes.

Knock knock.
Who's there?
Tori.
Tori who?
Tori I upset you.

Knock knock.
Who's there?
Tracy.
Tracy who?
Tracy the shape in pencil.

Knock knock.
Who's there?
Tricia.
Tricia who?
Bless you – what a bad cold!

Knock knock.
Who's there?
Trixie.
Trixie who?
Trixie played on you were really mean.

Knock knock.
Who's there?
Trudy.
Trudy who?
Trudy your word.

Knock knock.
Who's there?
Trudy.
Trudy who?
Trudy light from Turkey.

Knock knock.
Who's there?
Una.
Una who?
Yes, Una who.

Knock knock.
Who's there?
Utica.
Utica who?
(*sing*) "Utica high road and I'll take the low road."

Knock knock.
Who's there?
Val.
Val who?
Val, you really should know by now.

Knock knock.
Who's there?
Vanda.
Vanda who?
Vanda you vant me to come round?

Knock knock.
Who's there?
Vanessa.
Vanessa who?
Vanessa time I'll
  ring the bell.

Knock knock.
Who's there?
Viola.
Viola who?
Viola sudden you don't know who I am?

Knock knock.
Who's there?
Violet.
Violet who?
Violet the cat out of the bag.

Knock knock.
Who's there?
Wanda.
Wanda who?
Wanda new friend?

Knock knock.
Who's there?
Wendy.
Wendy who?
Wendy come to take you away I won't stop them!

Knock knock.
Who's there?
Whitney.
Whitney who?
Whitneyssed the crime.

Knock knock.
Who's there?
Wilhelmina.
Wilhelmina who?
Wilhelminan eternity in damnation?

Knock knock.
Who's there?
Willa.
Willa who?
Willa present make you happy?

Knock knock.
Who's there?
Winnie.
Winnie who?
Winnie is better than losing.

Chapter 2

Boys' names

Knock knock.
Who's there?
Chris.
Chris who?
Christmas stocking.

Knock knock.
Who's there?
Aaron.
Aaron who?
Aaron the chest means strength in the arms.

Knock knock.
Who's there?
Abel.
Abel who?
Abel to go to work.

Knock knock.
Who's there?
Abel.
Abel who?
Abel and a cow had a row.

Knock knock.
Who's there?
Adair.
Adair who?
Adair you to open this door.

Knock knock.
Who's there?
Adam.
Adam who?
Adam nuisance come to borrow some sugar.

Knock knock.
Who's there?
Adam.
Adam who?
Adam will burst any minute now.

Knock knock.
Who's there?
Adolph.
Adolph who?
Adolphin is a clever animal.

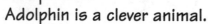

Knock knock.
Who's there?
Ahmed.
Ahmed who?
Ahmed a big mistake coming here!

Knock knock.
Who's there?
Al.
Al who?
Al be seeing you!

Knock knock.
Who's there?
Aladdin.
Aladdin who?
Aladdin short trousers.

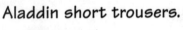

Knock knock.
Who's there?
Alan.
Alan who?
Alan a good cause.

Knock knock.
Who's there?
Alan.
Alan who?
Alantern will help you see in the dark.

Knock knock.
Who's there?
Albert.
Albert who?
Albert you'll never guess.

Knock knock.
Who's there?
Albert.
Albert who?
Alberta is in Canada.

Knock knock.
Who's there?
Aldo.
Aldo who?
Aldo the washing up tonight.

Knock knock.
Who's there?
Alec.
Alec who?
Alec your sister but I don't like you.

Knock knock.
Who's there?
Alex.
Alex who?
Alex plain later if you let me in.

Knock knock.
Who's there?
Alexander.
Alexander who?
Alexander friend want to come over.

Knock knock.
Who's there?
Alf.
Alf who?
Alf all if you don't catch me.

Knock knock.
Who's there?
Alf.
Alf who?
Alf way home.

Knock knock.
Who's there?
Alfie.
Alfie who?
Alfie terrible if you leave.

Knock knock.
Who's there?
Alfie.
Alfie who?
Alfieed the animals if I want to.

Knock knock.
Who's there?
Alistair.
Alistair who?
Alistairs in this house are broken.

Knock knock.
Who's there?
Alvin.
Alvin who?
Alvin zis competition – just vait and see!

Knock knock.
Who's there?
Amin.
Amin who?
Amin man.

Knock knock.
Who's there?
Amos.
Amos who?
Amos be mad! This isn't my house.

Knock knock.
Who's there?
Amos.
Amos who?
Amosquito.

Knock knock.
Who's there?
Andrew.
Andrew who?
Andrew a picture on the wall.

Knock knock.
Who's there?
Andy.
Andy who?
Andy man.

Knock knock.
Who's there?
Angus.
Angus who?
Angus us to see
 such cruelty.

Knock knock.
Who's there?
Archibald.
Archibald who?
Archibald, but Arthur wears a wig.

Knock knock.
Who's there?
Archie.
Archie who?
Archieeses always smelly?

Knock knock.
Who's there?
Armand.
Armand who?
Armand icing is marzipan.

Knock knock.
Who's there?
Armstrong.
Armstrong who?
Armstronger than you are.

Knock knock.
Who's there?
Arnie.
Arnie who?
Arnie going to let me in?

Knock knock.
Who's there?
Arnold.
Arnold who?
Arnold man.

Knock knock.
Who's there?
Asa.
Asa who?
Asa glass of orange out of the question?

Knock knock.
Who's there?
Atlas.
Atlas who?
Atlas Vegas you can gamble all night.

Knock knock.
Who's there?
Attila.
Attila who?
Attila you no lies.

Knock knock.
Who's there?
Augustine.
Augustine who?
Augustine Greece is too hot.

Knock knock.
Who's there?
Austin.
Austin who?
Austintatiously rich.

Knock knock.
Who's there?
Barney.
Barney who?
Barneyded for thirsty man.

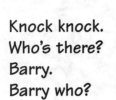

Knock knock.
Who's there?
Barry.
Barry who?
Barry the dead.

Knock knock.
Who's there?
Bart.
Bart who?
Bartender or beer-drinker?

Knock knock.
Who's there?
Ben.
Ben who?
Ben down and tie your shoelaces.

Knock knock.
Who's there?
Ben and Anna.
Ben and Anna who?
Ben and Anna split.

Knock knock.
Who's there?
Benedict.
Benedict who?
Ben 'e dictated all his letters.

Knock knock.
Who's there?
Benjamin.
Benjamin who.
Benjamin the blues.

Knock knock.
Who's there?
Bernard.
Bernard who?
Bernardly anything to cut fuel bills.

Knock knock.
Who's there?
Bernie.
Bernie who?
Bernie bridges.

Knock knock.
Who's there?
Bert.
Bert who?
Bert the cakes.

Knock knock.
Who's there?
Bill.
Bill who?
Bill of rights.

Knock knock.
Who's there?
Bjorn.
Bjorn who?
Bjorn free.

Knock knock.
Who's there?
Blake.
Blake who?
Blake and white.

Knock knock.
Who's there?
Bobby.
Bobby who?
Bobbyn up and down like this.

Knock knock.
Who's there?
Boris.
Boris who?
Boristol City or Bristol Rovers?

Knock knock.
Who's there?
Brad.
Brad who?
Brad to meet ya!

Knock knock.
Who's there?
Bradley.
Bradley who?
Bradley in need of repair.

Knock knock.
Who's there?
Brian.
Brian who?
Brian drain!

Knock knock.
Who's there?
Brendan.
Brendan who?
Brendan ear to what I have to say.

Knock knock.
Who's there?
Brett.
Brett who?
Bretter late than never.

Knock knock.
Who's there?
Brock.
Brock who?
Brockfast in bed.

Knock knock.
Who's there?
Bruce.
Bruce who?
Bruce easily with soft skin.

Knock knock.
Who's there?
Bruno.
Bruno who?
Bruno more tea for me.

Knock knock.
Who's there?
Buster.
Buster who?
Buster the town, please.

Knock knock.
Who's there?
Buster.
Buster who?
Buster blood vessel.

Knock knock.
Who's there?
Caesar.
Caesar who?
Caesar jolly good fellow.

Knock knock.
Who's there?
Cain.
Cain who?
Cain tell you.

Knock knock.
Who's there?
Callum.
Callum who?
Callum all back.

Knock knock.
Who's there?
Carl.
Carl who?
Carl you see?

Knock knock.
Who's there?
Carlo.
Carlo who?
Carload of people to see you.

Knock knock.
Who's there?
Carlos.
Carlos who?
Carlossal cheek to do such a thing.

Knock knock.
Who's there?
Charles.
Charles who?
Charles your luck on the roulette wheel.

Knock knock.
Who's there?
Chester.
Chester who?
Chester minute! Don't you know who I am?

Knock knock.
Who's there?
Chester.
Chester who?
Chester drawers.

Knock knock.
Who's there?
Chuck.
Chuck who?
Chuck in a sandwich for lunch!

Knock knock.
Who's there?
Clarence.
Clarence who?
Clarence sale.

Knock knock.
Who's there?
Clay.
Clay who?
Clay on, Sam.

Knock knock.
Who's there?
Clifford.
Clifford who?
Cliffordered the jelly and ice cream.

Knock knock.
Who's there?
Cliff.
Cliff who?
Cliffhanger.

Knock knock.
Who's there?
Cohen.
Cohen who?
Cohen your way.

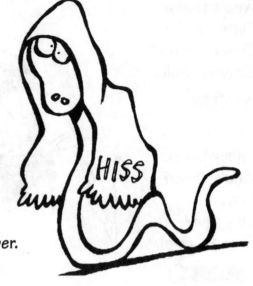

Knock knock.
Who's there?
Cole.
Cole who?
Cole as a cucumber.

Knock knock.
Who's there?
Colin.
Colin who?
Colin all cars ... Colin all cars ...

Knock knock.
Who's there?
Colin.
Colin who?
Colin and see me next time you're passing.

Knock knock.
Who's there?
Connor.
Connor who?
Connor long way past my turning.

Knock knock.
Who's there?
Conrad.
Conrad who?
Conrad with embarrassment.

Knock knock.
Who's there?
Cosmo.
Cosmo who?
Cosmo trouble than you're worth.

Knock knock.
Who's there?
Costas.
Costas who?
Costas a fortune to get here.

Knock knock.
Who's there?
Craig.
Craig who?
Craig in the wall.

Knock knock.
Who's there?
Craig.
Craig who?
Craigy mountain
ranges.

Knock knock.
Who's there?
Crispin.
Crispin who?
Crispin crunchy is how I like my cereal.

Knock knock.
Who's there?
Curtis.
Curtis who?
Curtisey is a sign of good upbringing.

Knock knock.
Who's there?
Cyril.
Cyril who?
Cyril animals at the zoo.

Knock knock.
Who's there?
Dale.
Dale who?
Dale come if you call dem.

Knock knock.
Who's there?
Danny.
Danny who?
Dannybody home?

Knock knock.
Who's there?
Darren.
Darren who?
Darren the garden, hiding.

Knock knock.
Who's there?
Dave.
Dave who?
Dave of glory.

Knock knock.
Who's there?
Dave.
Dave who?
Dave-andalised
 our home.

Knock knock.
Who's there?
Derek.
Derek who?
Derek get richer and the poor get poorer.

Knock knock.
Who's there?
Derek.
Derek who?
Derektly outside your door.

Knock knock.
Who's there?
Dermot.
Dermot who?
Dermotology is only skin deep.

Knock knock.
Who's there?
Desi.
Desi who?
Desi take sugar?

Knock knock.
Who's there?
Devlin.
Devlin who?
Devlin a red dress.

Knock knock.
Who's there?
Dewey.
Dewey who?
Dewey stay or do we go now?

Knock knock.
Who's there?
Dick.
Dick who?
Dicktate your name more slowly.

Knock knock.
Who's there?
Diego.
Diego who?
Diego before de "B".

Knock knock.
Who's there?
Don.
Don who?
Don take me for granted.

Knock knock.
Who's there?
Donovan.
Donovan who?
Donovan the door, it's dangerous.

Knock knock.
Who's there?
Dougal.
Dougal who?
Dougals nest on cliffs?

Knock knock.
Who's there?
Douglas.
Douglas who?
Douglas is broken.

Knock knock.
Who's there?
Duane.
Duane who?
Duane gonna get away with dis!

Knock knock.
Who's there?
Duke.
Duke who?
Duke come here often?

Knock knock.
Who's there?
Duncan.
Duncan who?
Duncanada, now I'm off to Japan.

Knock knock.
Who's there?
Duncan.
Duncan who?
Duncan biscuit in your tea.

Knock knock.
Who's there?
Duncan.
Duncan who?
Duncan make your garden grow.

Knock knock.
Who's there?
Dwight.
Dwight who?
Dwight house is where the President lives.

Knock knock.
Who's there?
Eamon.
Eamon who?
Eamon a good mood – have my piece of cake.

Knock knock.
Who's there?
Eamon.
Eamon who?
Eamon to please.

Knock knock.
Who's there?
Earl.
Earl who?
Earl tell you if you open the door.

Knock knock.
Who's there?
Earl.
Earl who?
Earl abuse and you'll get more in return.

Knock knock.
Who's there?
Eddie.
Eddie who?
Eddie-body you like.

Knock knock.
Who's there?
Edward.
Edward who?
Edward like to play now, please.

Knock knock.
Who's there?
Edwin.
Edwin who?
Edwin a cup if I could run faster.

Knock knock.
Who's there?
Egbert.
Egbert who?
Egbert no bacon.

Knock knock.
Who's there?
Eli.
Eli who?
Eli, eli, oh!

Knock knock.
Who's there?
Eli.
Eli who?
Elies all the time.

Knock knock.
Who's there?
Ellis.
Ellis who?
Ellis damnation.

Knock knock.
Who's there?
Emil.
Emil who?
Emil would be nice if you've got some food.

Knock knock.
Who's there?
Emile.
Emile who?
Emileitary escort.

Knock knock.
Who's there?
Emmett.
Emmett who?
Emmett the front door, not the back.

Knock knock.
Who's there?
Emrys.
Emrys who?
Emrysking everything to be here.

Knock knock.
Who's there?
Enoch.
Enoch who?
Enochulate to prevent the spread of disease.

Knock knock.
Who's there?
Eric.
Eric who?
Ericshaw driver.

Knock knock.
Who's there?
Ernest.
Ernest who?
Ernest is made from twigs.

Knock knock.
Who's there?
Esau.
Esau who?
Esau you in the bath!

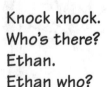

Knock knock.
Who's there?
Ethan.
Ethan who?
Ethan all my dinner.

Knock knock.
Who's there?
Ethan.
Ethan who?
Ethan people don't go to church.

Knock knock.
Who's there?
Eugene.
Eugene who?
Eugene, me Tarzan.

Knock knock.
Who's there?
Evan.
Evan who?
Evan only knows!

Knock knock.
Who's there?
Ewan.
Ewan who?
Ewan me should get together.

Knock knock.
Who's there?
Ezra.
Ezra who?
Ezra room to rent?

Knock knock.
Who's there?
Felipe.
Felipe who?
Felipe a bath – I need a wash!

Knock knock.
Who's there?
Felix.
Felix who?
Felixtremely cold.

Knock knock.
Who's there?
Felix.
Felix who?
Felix my face again I'll give him a smack.

Knock knock.
Who's there?
Fido.
Fido who?
Fido known you were coming I'd have baked a cake.

Knock knock.
Who's there?
Fletcher.
Fletcher who?
Fletcher stick, there's a good boy.

Knock knock.
Who's there?
Foster.
Foster who?
Foster than a speeding bullet.

Knock knock.
Who's there?
Francis.
Francis who?
Francis where the French live.

Knock knock.
Who's there?
Frank.
Frank who?
Frank you very much.

Knock knock.
Who's there?
Frankie.
Frankie who?
Frankie speaking, it's awful.

Knock knock.
Who's there?
Franz.
Franz who?
Franz, Romans, countrymen, lend me your ears.

Knock knock.
Who's there?
Fraser.
Fraser who?
Fraser jolly good fellow!

Knock knock.
Who's there?
Fred.
Fred who?
Fred this needle – I'm cross-eyed.

Knock knock.
Who's there?
Freddie.
Freddie who?
Freddie won't come out to play today.

Knock knock.
Who's there?
Freddie and Abel.
Freddie and Abel who?
Freddie and Abel
  to do business.

Knock knock.
Who's there?
Gary.
Gary who?
Gary on smiling.

Knock knock.
Who's there?
Geoff.
Geoff who?
Geoff feel like going out tonight?

Knock knock.
Who's there?
Gerald.
Gerald who?
Gerald man from round the corner.

Knock knock.
Who's there?
Gervase.
Gervase who?
Gervaseting my time.

Knock knock.
Who's there?
Gideon.
Gideon who?
Gideon my feet, I've drunk too much.

Knock knock.
Who's there?
Giovanni.
Giovanni who?
Giovanninny more coffee?

Knock knock.
Who's there?
Giuseppe.
Giuseppe who?
Giuseppe credit cards?

Knock knock.
Who's there?
Gordon.
Gordon who?
Gordon bleu chef.

Knock knock.
Who's there?
Grant.
Grant who?
Grant three wishes.

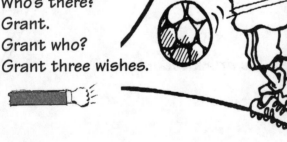

Knock knock.
Who's there?
Greg.
Greg who?
Greg Scott!

Knock knock.
Who's there?
Gus.
Gus who?
Gus what – it's me!

Knock knock.
Who's there?
Guthrie.
Guthrie who?
Guthrie ice-creams in my hand.

Knock knock.
Who's there?
Guy.
Guy who?
Guy do you ask?

Knock knock.
Who's there?
Hal.
Hal who?
Hal for leather.

Knock knock.
Who's there?
Hamish.
Hamish who?
Hamishter, ish thish the way to Shalishbury?

Knock knock.
Who's there?
Hank.
Hank who?
Hank you for asking.

Knock knock.
Who's there?
Hans.
Hans who?
Hans across the sea.

Knock knock.
Who's there?
Hardy.
Hardy who?
Hardy annual.

Knock knock.
Who's there?
Harry.
Harry who?
Harry up!

Knock knock.
Who's there?
Harry.
Harry who?
Harrycot beans or runner beans for you?

Knock knock.
Who's there?
Hayden.
Hayden who?
Hayden behind the door.

Knock knock.
Who's there?
Herman.
Herman who?
Herman dry.

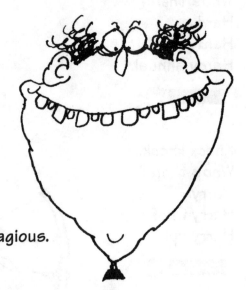

Knock knock.
Who's there?
Hermes.
Hermes who?
Hermesles are contagious.

Knock knock.
Who's there?
Heywood.
Heywood who?
Heywood you open the door?

Knock knock.
Who's there?
Hiram.
Hiram who?
Hiram and fire 'em.

Knock knock.
Who's there?
Horatio.
Horatio who?
Horatio to the end of the road.

Knock knock.
Who's there?
Howard.
Howard who?
Howard you know? You won't even open up.

Knock knock.
Who's there?
Howard.
Howard who?
Howard are diamonds?

Knock knock.
Who's there?
Howie.
Howie who?
Fine thanks. How are you?

Knock knock.
Who's there?
Huey.
Huey who?
Who am I? I'm me!

Knock knock.
Who's there?
Hugh.
Hugh who?
Hugh wouldn't believe it if I told you.

Knock knock.
Who's there?
Hugo.
Hugo who?
Hugoing away this summer?

Knock knock.
Who's there?
Humphrey.
Humphrey who?
Humphrey, but there is a charge for signing.

Knock knock.
Who's there?
Ian.
Ian who?
Ian a lot of money.

Knock knock.
Who's there?
Ike.
Ike who?
Ike'n see you through the keyhole.

Knock knock.
Who's there?
Ira.
Ira who?
Irate – or I will be if I stand out here any longer!

Knock knock.
Who's there?
Isaac.
Isaac who?
Isaac all my staff today.

Knock knock.
Who's there?
Isaac.
Isaac who?
Isaac my thumb when I'm nervous.

Knock knock.
Who's there?
Ivan.
Ivan who?
Ivan enormous snake in my pocket.

Knock knock.
Who's there?
Ivan.
Ivan who?
Ivangered you again, haven't I?

Knock knock.
Who's there?
Ivor.
Ivor who?
Ivor lot more jokes where
 this came from!

Knock knock.
Who's there?
Jack.
Jack who?
Jack in the box.

Knock knock.
Who's there?
James.
James who?
James people play.

Knock knock.
Who's there?
Jamie.
Jamie who?
Jamie'n you don't recognise my voice?

Knock knock.
Who's there?
Jason.
Jason who?
Jason a rainbow.

Knock knock.
Who's there?
Jay.
Jay who?
Jay what you mean.

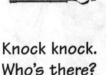

Knock knock.
Who's there?
Jeff.
Jeff who?
Jeff fancy going out tonight?

Knock knock.
Who's there?
Jeffrey.
Jeffrey who?
Jeffrey time I knock, you ask who I am.

Knock knock.
Who's there?
Jerome.
Jerome who?
Jerome alone.

Knock knock.
Who's there?
Jerry.
Jerry who?
Jerry cake?

Knock knock.
Who's there?
Jess.
Jess who?
Don't know, you tell me.

Knock knock.
Who's there?
Jesse.
Jesse who?
Jesse if you can recognise my voice.

Knock knock.
Who's there?
Jethro.
Jethro who?
Jethro our ball back, please.

Knock knock.
Who's there?
Jez.
Jez who?
Jezt a minute.

Knock knock.
Who's there?
Jim.
Jim who?
Jim mind if we come and stay with you?

Knock knock.
Who's there?
Jimmy.
Jimmy who?
Jimmy all your money.

Knock knock.
Who's there?
Jimmy.
Jimmy who?
Jimmytate any famous personalities?

Knock knock.
Who's there?
Jock.
Jock who?
Jockupy this house on your own?

Knock knock.
Who's there?
Joe.
Joe who?
Joe away – I'm not talking to you.

Knock knock.
Who's there?
Johan.
Johan who?
Johandsome beast!

Knock knock.
Who's there?
Johann.
Johann who?
Johann! How you doing, dude!

Knock knock.
Who's there?
John.
John who?
John in the fun.

Knock knock.
Who's there?
Jonah.
Jonah who?
Jonah bicycle?

Knock knock.
Who's there?
Joseph.
Joseph who?
Josephicient at doing nothing.

Knock knock.
Who's there?
Juan.
Juan who?
Just Juan of those things.

Knock knock.
Who's there?
Juan.
Juan who?
Juance upon a time there were three bears...

Knock knock.
Who's there?
Judas.
Judas who?
Judash about like this all the time?

Knock knock.
Who's there?
Jude.
Jude who?
Jude doubt me?
Just open up.

Knock knock.
Who's there?
Julian.
Julian who?
Juliand I are going shopping now.

Knock knock.
Who's there?
Julian.
Julian who?
Julian a mattress?

Knock knock.
Who's there?
Justin.
Justin who?
Justin time.

Knock knock.
Who's there?
Keith.
Keith who?
Keith your hands off me!

Knock knock.
Who's there?
Ken.
Ken who?
Ken you come and play?

156

Knock knock.
Who's there?
Kenneth.
Kenneth who?
Kenneth three little kittens come out to play?

Knock knock.
Who's there?
Kevin.
Kevin who?
Kevin and sit down.

Knock knock.
Who's there?
Kevin.
Kevin who?
Kevin it all you've got.

Knock knock.
Who's there?
Kit.
Kit who?
Kit out of it!

Knock knock.
Who's there?
Kurt.
Kurt who?
Kurt and wounded.

Knock knock.
Who's there?
Kyle.
Kyle who?
Kyle be good if you let me in!

Knock knock.
Who's there?
Larry.
Larry who?
Larry up.

Knock knock.
Who's there?
Laurie.
Laurie who?
Laurie-load of goods.

Knock knock.
Who's there?
Len.
Len who?
Len us a fiver will you?

Knock knock.
Who's there?
Leon.
Leon who?
Leon me – I'll support you.

Knock knock.
Who's there?
Les.
Les who?
Les see what we can do.

Knock knock.
Who's there?
Lester.
Lester who?
Lester we forget.

Knock knock.
Who's there?
Lewis.
Lewis who?
Lewis all my money in a poker game.

Knock knock.
Who's there?
Lewis.
Lewis who?
Lewist form of life.

Knock knock.
Who's there?
Lionel.
Lionel who?
Lionel roar if you stand on its tail.

Knock knock.
Who's there?
Lionel.
Lionel who?
Lionel find out the truth anyway.

Knock knock.
Who's there?
Llewellyn.
Llewellyn who?
Llewellyn with the management.

Knock knock.
Who's there?
Lloyd.
Lloyd who?
Lloyd him away with an ice-cream.

Knock knock.
Who's there?
Lou.
Lou who?
Lou's your money on the horses.

Knock knock.
Who's there?
Lucas.
Lucas who?
Lucas sweet as you can.

Knock knock.
Who's there?
Luke.
Luke who?
Luke through the peep-hole and you'll see.

Knock knock.
Who's there?
Luther.
Luther who?
Luther please – not tho tight!

Knock knock.
Who's there?
Lyle.
Lyle who?
Lyle low until the cops have gone.

Knock knock.
Who's there?
Malcolm.
Malcolm who?
Malcolm outside and play!

Knock knock.
Who's there?
Malone.
Malone who?
Malonely heart is aching.

Knock knock.
Who's there?
Marcus.
Marcus who?
Marcus a really nice boy.

Knock knock.
Who's there?
Marcus.
Marcus who?
Marcus in, I've forgotten my pen.

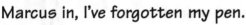

Knock knock.
Who's there?
Mark.
Mark who?
Mark my words.

Knock knock.
Who's there?
Marshall.
Marshall who?
Marshall arts can be dangerous.

Knock knock.
Who's there?
Martin.
Martin who?
Martin to be in goal.

Knock knock.
Who's there?
Marvin.
Marvin who?
Marvin at these amazing tricks.

Knock knock.
Who's there?
Matt.
Matt who?
Mattinee idol the ladies love.

Knock knock.
Who's there?
Matthew.
Matthew who?
Matthew always thpeak with a listhp?

Knock knock.
Who's there?
Max.
Max who?
Max headroom.

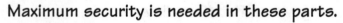

Knock knock.
Who's there?
Max.
Max who?
Maximum security is needed in these parts.

Knock knock.
Who's there?
Maximilian.
Maximilian who?
Maximiliannaire look poor!

Knock knock.
Who's there?
Maxwell.
Maxwell who?
Maxwell, but Jock's ill.

Knock knock.
Who's there?
Mel.
Mel who?
Melt down!

Knock knock.
Who's there?
Merlin.
Merlin who?
Merlingering with a fictitious illness.

Knock knock.
Who's there?
Michael.
Michael who?
Michaelock has stopped ticking.

Knock knock.
Who's there?
Mike.
Mike who?
Mike the best of it.

Knock knock.
Who's there?
Mike.
Mike who?
Mike-andle's just blown out. It's all dark.

Knock knock.
Who's there?
Mike and Angelo.
Mike and Angelo who?
Mike and Angelo's *David*.

Knock knock.
Who's there?
Mikey.
Mikey who?
Mikey is stuck.

Knock knock.
Who's there?
Miles.
Miles who?
Miles away.

Knock knock.
Who's there?
Milo.
Milo who?
Milo bed is too uncomfortable.

Knock knock.
Who's there?
Misha.
Misha who?
Misha lot of things
  while I was away?

Knock knock.
Who's there?
Monty.
Monty who?
Monty Carlo or bust.

Knock knock.
Who's there?
Mordecai.
Mordecai who?
Mordecai, said the dentist – too many sweets.

Knock knock.
Who's there?
Moses.
Moses who?
Moses lawn with a hover mower.

Knock knock.
Who's there?
Murphy.
Murphy who?
Murphy, murphy me!

Knock knock.
Who's there?
Murray.
Murray who?
Murray me now.

Knock knock.
Who's there?
Nat.
Nat who?
Nat going to tell you!

Knock knock.
Who's there?
Ned.
Ned who?
Neducation is what you get at school.

Knock knock.
Who's there?
Neil.
Neil who?
Neil down and pray.

Knock knock.
Who's there?
Nicholas.
Nicholas who?
Nicholas girls shouldn't
 climb trees.

Knock knock.
Who's there?
Nicholas.
Nicholas who?
Nicholas and nip a lad.

Knock knock.
Who's there?
Nick.
Nick who?
Nick R. Elastic.

Knock knock.
Who's there?
Noah.
Noah who?
Noah don't know who you are either.

Knock knock.
Who's there?
Noel.
Noel who?
Noel life, that's your problem.

Knock knock.
Who's there?
Norman.
Norman who?
Norman behaviour is expected here.

Knock knock.
Who's there?
Norris.
Norris who?
Norrisk if you play safely.

Knock knock.
Who's there?
Oberon.
Oberon who?
Oberon the other side of the road.

Knock knock.
Who's there?
Oedipus.
Oedipus who?
Oedipus in the
  swimming pool.

Knock knock.
Who's there?
Oliver.
Oliver who?
Oliver all my money in my will.

Knock knock.
Who's there?
Oliver.
Oliver who?
Oliver long way away.

Knock knock.
Who's there?
Oliver.
Oliver who?
Oliver lone and I'm afraid.

Knock knock.
Who's there?
Omar.
Omar who?
Omar goodness, what are you doing in there?

Knock knock.
Who's there?
Orson.
Orson who?
Orson, let your daddy in.

Knock knock.
Who's there?
Oscar.
Oscar who?
Oscar a foolish question, get a foolish answer.

Knock knock.
Who's there?
Oswald.
Oswald who?
Oswald in like an old garden.

Knock knock.
Who's there?
Othello.
Othello who?
Othello I wouldn't trust an inch.

Knock knock.
Who's there?
Owen.
Owen who?
Owen up, we all know you did it.

Knock knock.
Who's there?
Pablo.
Pablo who?
Pablo the candles out.

Knock knock.
Who's there?
Paddy.
Paddy who?
Paddy'd about his cell like a caged animal.

Knock knock.
Who's there?
Patrick.
Patrick who?
Patricked me into coming.

Knock knock.
Who's there?
Paul.
Paul who?
Paul up a chair and I'll tell you.

Knock knock.
Who's there?
Pedro.
Pedro who?
Pedrol prices keep going up.

Knock knock.
Who's there?
Percy.
Percy who?
Percy Verence is the secret of success.

Knock knock.
Who's there?
Percy.
Percy who?
Percycuted for a crime I didn't commit.

Knock knock.
Who's there?
Perry.
Perry who?
Perry well, thank you.

Knock knock.
Who's there?
Peter.
Peter who?
Peter cake.

Knock knock.
Who's there?
Peter Pan.
Peter Pan who?
Peter Panting after a long race.

Knock knock.
Who's there?
Philip.
Philip who?
Philip the car with petrol.

Knock knock.
Who's there?
Pierre.
Pierre who?
Pierre through the keyhole – you'll see.

Knock knock.
Who's there?
Piers.
Piers who?
Piers are the
   aristocracy.

Knock knock.
Who's there?
Puck.
Puck who?
Puck up your troubles in your old kit bag.

Knock knock.
Who's there?
Ralph.
Ralph who?
Ralph, ralph – I'm just a puppy.

Knock knock.
Who's there?
Ralph.
Ralph who?
Ralphabetically, I'm way down the list.

Knock knock.
Who's there?
Raoul.
Raoul who?
Raoul of law.

Knock knock.
Who's there?
Ray.
Ray who?
Rayn drops keep falling on my head.

Knock knock.
Who's there?
Raymond.
Raymond who?
Raymond me to take that book back.

Knock knock.
Who's there?
Rees.
Rees who?
Reesembles a monkey.

Knock knock.
Who's there?
Reuben.
Reuben who?
Reuben my eyes.

Knock knock.
Who's there?
Rex.
Rex who?
Rex may be full of sunken treasure.

Knock knock.
Who's there?
Rhys.
Rhys who?
Rhysky to cross the road here.

Knock knock.
Who's there?
Richard.
Richard who?
Richard poor have little in common.

Knock knock.
Who's there?
Robert.
Robert who?
Roberts are taking over the world.

Knock knock.
Who's there?
Robin.
Robin who?
Robin banks.

Knock knock.
Who's there?
Roddy.
Roddy who?
Roddy rotten trick to play on anyone.

Knock knock.
Who's there?
Roland.
Roland who?
Roland butter please.

Knock knock.
Who's there?
Roland.
Roland who?
Roland stone gathers no moss.

Knock knock.
Who's there?
Rolf.
Rolf who?
Rolfor a six to start the game.

Knock knock.
Who's there?
Romeo.
Romeo who?
Romeover the river.

Knock knock.
Who's there?
Ron.
Ron who?
Ron way round.

Knock knock.
Who's there?
Ronnie.
Ronnie who?
Ronnie butter spreads more easily.

Knock knock.
Who's there?
Ross.
Ross who?
Rosstle up a few more people.

Knock knock.
Who's there?
Rudi.
Rudi who?
Rudi toot!

Knock knock.
Who's there?
Russ.
Russ who?
Russian tea is served with a slice of lemon.

Knock knock.
Who's there?
Russell.
Russell who?
Russelling leaves.

Knock knock.
Who's there?
Sam.
Sam who?
Sam day you'll recognise my voice.

Knock knock.
Who's there?
Sam.
Sam who?
Samazing, that's who it is.

Knock knock.
Who's there?
Samuel.
Samuel who?
Samuel win, some you'll lose.

Knock knock.
Who's there?
Sancho.
Sancho who?
Sanchovy paste I like the best.

Knock knock.
Who's there?
Saul.
Saul who?
Saul I know.

Knock knock.
Who's there?
Saul.
Saul who?
Saul over and done with.

Knock knock.
Who's there?
Scott.
Scott who?
Scott nothing to do with you.

Knock knock.
Who's there?
Scott.
Scott who?
Scott land the brave.

Knock knock.
Who's there?
Seamus.
Seamus who?
Seamus into confessing.

Knock knock.
Who's there?
Sebastian.
Sebastian who?
Sebastian of society.

Knock knock.
Who's there?
Serge.
Serge who?
Serge high and low.

Knock knock.
Who's there?
Seymour.
Seymour who?
Seymour from the top window.

Knock knock.
Who's there?
Shane.
Shane who?
Shane and shenshible.

Knock knock.
Who's there?
Sid.
Sid who?
Sid on it!

Knock knock.
Who's there?
Sid.
Sid who?
Sidiotic question!

Knock knock.
Who's there?
Simon.
Simon who?
Simon time again I've told you not to do that.

Knock knock.
Who's there?
Sinbad.
Sinbad who?
Sinbad shape for his age.

Knock knock.
Who's there?
Solomon.
Solomon who?
Solomon this sombre occasion.

Knock knock.
Who's there?
Stan.
Stan who?
Stand back, I'm going to be sick.

Knock knock.
Who's there?
Stan and Della.
Stan and Della who?
Stan and Dellaver.

Knock knock.
Who's there?
Stefan.
Stefan who?
Stefan it!

Knock knock.
Who's there?
Stefan.
Stefan who?
Stefaning when you play the drums.

Knock knock.
Who's there?
Steve.
Steve who?
Steve upper lip.

Knock knock.
Who's there?
Stevie.
Stevie who.
Stevie has a terrible reception.

Knock knock.
Who's there?
Talbot.
Talbot who?
Talbot too thin.

Knock knock.
Who's there?
Terence.
Terence who?
Terence of rain caused the flooding.

Knock knock.
Who's there?
Terry.
Terry who?
Terryble twins or tricky triplets?

Knock knock.
Who's there?
Theo.
Theo who?
Theold Curiosity Shop.

Knock knock.
Who's there?
Theodore.
Theodore who?
Theodore is locked.

Knock knock.
Who's there?
Theodore.
Theodore who?
Theodore is terrible – what a pong!

Knock knock.
Who's there?
Thomas.
Thomas who?
Thomaster a language takes a long time.

Knock knock.
Who's there?
Thor.
Thor who?
Thort I saw you were in.

Knock knock.
Who's there?
Tim.
Tim who?
Tim after time.

Knock knock.
Who's there?
Tim.
Tim who?
Timpossible to tell you.

Knock knock.
Who's there?
Tito.
Tito who?
Titotal people don't drink alcohol.

Knock knock.
Who's there?
Tobias.
Tobias who?
Tobias all presents will cost a fortune.

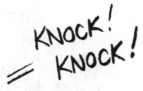

Knock knock.
Who's there?
Toby.
Toby who?
Toby or not Toby, that is the question.

Knock knock.
Who's there?
Todd.
Todd who?
Toddle off and don't come back.

Knock knock.
Who's there?
Tom.
Tom who?
Tomato soup.

Knock knock.
Who's there?
Tom Sawyer.
Tom Sawyer who?
Tom Sawyer at it again!

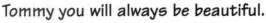

Knock knock.
Who's there?
Tommy.
Tommy who?
Tommy you will always be beautiful.

Knock knock.
Who's there?
Tristan.
Tristan who?
Tristan elephant not to forget.

Knock knock.
Who's there?
Tristan.
Tristan who?
Tristan shout.

Knock knock.
Who's there?
Troy.
Troy who?
Troy the bell instead.

Knock knock.
Who's there?
Uriah.
Uriah who?
Uriah than I am in the ratings.

Knock knock.
Who's there?
Van.
Van who?
Van I vant you, I'll let you know.

Knock knock.
Who's there?
Vaughan.
Vaughan who?
Vaughan out by too much work.

Knock knock.
Who's there?
Vernon.
Vernon who?
Vernon-smokers only, this carriage!

Knock knock.
Who's there?
Vic.
Vic who?
Victory parade.

Knock knock.
Who's there?
Vic.
Vic who?
Victim of a vampire.

Knock knock.
Who's there?
Vincent.
Vincent who?
Vincent me here.

Knock knock.
Who's there?
Wade.
Wade who?
Wading room.

Knock knock.
Who's there?
Wallis.
Wallis who?
Wallis can be expected.

Knock knock.
Who's there?
Walter.
Walter who?
Walter, walter everywhere and not a drop to drink.

Knock knock.
Who's there?
Walter.
Walter who?
Walter wall carpeting.

Knock knock.
Who's there?
Ward.
Ward who?
Ward you want?

Knock knock.
Who's there?
Warren.
Warren who?
Warren Peace, by Tolstoy.

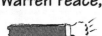

Knock knock.
Who's there?
Wayne.
Wayne who?
(sing) "Wayne in a manger, no crib for a bed."

Knock knock.
Who's there?
Webster.
Webster who?
Webster a spider are easily spun.

Knock knock.
Who's there?
Wesley.
Wesley who?
Wesley wind is
  blowing out here.

Knock knock.
Who's there?
Wilbur.
Wilbur who?
Wilburn fireworks on November 5th.

Knock knock.
Who's there?
Wilfred.
Wilfred who?
Wilfred come if we ask nicely?

Chapter 3

Rich and famous

Knock knock.
Who's there?
Ben Hur.
Ben Hur who?
Ben Hur an hour – let me in.

Knock knock.
Who's there?
Abba.
Abba who?
Abba'out turn! Quick march!

Knock knock.
Who's there?
Aesop.
Aesop who?
Aesop I saw a pussycat.

Knock knock.
Who's there?
Amin.
Amin who?
Amin thing to do.

Knock knock.
Who's there?
Anka.
Anka who?
Anka the ship.

Knock knock.
Who's there?
Aretha.
Aretha who?
Aretha flowers.

Knock knock.
Who's there?
Atlas.
Atlas who?
Atlas you opened the door.

Knock knock.
Who's there?
Attila.
Attila who?
Attila you no lies.

Knock knock.
Who's there?
Austen.
Austen who?
Austen corrected.

Knock knock.
Who's there?
Axl.
Axl who?
Axl me nicely and I'll tell you.

Knock knock.
Who's there?
Bach.
Bach who?
Bach to work.

Knock knock.
Who's there?
Becker.
Becker who?
Becker the devil you know.

Knock knock.
Who's there?
Beethoven.
Beethoven who?
Beethoven is too hot!

Knock knock.
Who's there?
Ben Hur.
Ben Hur who?
Ben Hur an hour – let me in.

Knock knock.
Who's there?
Bjork.
Bjork who?
Bjork in the USSR.

Knock knock.
Who's there?
Blair.
Blair who?
Blair play.

Knock knock.
Who's there?
Blur.
Blur who?
Blur! It's cold out here.

Knock knock.
Who's there?
Bolton.
Bolton who?
Bolton the door.

Knock knock.
Who's there?
Borg.
Borg who?
Borg standard.

Knock knock.
Who's there?
Boyzone.
Boyzone who?
Boyzone adventures.

Knock knock
Who's there?
Bronte.
Bronte who?
Bronte of the blow.

Knock knock.
Who's there?
Burns.
Burns who?
Burns me up.

Knock knock.
Who's there?
Bush.
Bush who?
Bush your money where your mouth is.

Knock knock.
Who's there?
Byron.
Byron who?
Byron new suit.

Knock knock.
Who's there?
Caesar.
Caesar who?
Caesar arm to stop her getting away.

Knock knock.
Who's there?
Castro.
Castro who?
Castro bread upon the waters.

Knock knock.
Who's there?
Cher.
Cher who?
Cher and share alike!

Knock knock.
Who's there?
Chopin.
Chopin who?
Chopin the department store.

Knock knock.
Who's there?
Churchill.
Churchill who?
Churchill be the best place for your wedding.

Knock knock.
Who's there?
Cicero.
Cicero who?
Cicero the boat ashore.

Knock knock.
Who's there?
Clinton.
Clinton who?
Clinton your eye.

Knock knock.
Who's there?
Coolidge.
Coolidge who?
Coolidge a cucumber.

Knock knock.
Who's there?
Cronkite.
Cronkite who?
Cronkite evidence.

Knock knock.
Who's there?
Dali.
Dali who?
Dali've me alone.

Knock knock.
Who's there?
Demi Moore.
Demi Moore who?
Demi Moore than you did last time.

Knock knock.
Who's there?
De Niro.
De Niro who?
De Niro you get, the faster I run.

Knock knock.
Who's there?
Debussy.
Debussy who?
Debussy's never on time.

Knock knock.
Who's there?
Depp.
Depp who?
Depp inside dear!

Knock knock.
Who's there?
Diaz.
Diaz who?
Diaz of our lives.

Knock knock.
Who's there?
Dimaggio.
Dimaggio who?
Dimaggio yourself on a deserted island ...

Knock knock.
Who's there?
Doctor.
Doctor Who?
That's right – where's my Tardis?

Knock knock.
Who's there?
Donatello.
Donatello who?
Donatellon me.

Knock knock.
Who's there?
Eisenhower.
Eisenhower who?
Eisenhower late for work.

Knock knock.
Who's there?
Elton.
Elton who?
Elton old lady, please.

Knock knock.
Who's there?
Elvis.
Elvis who?
Elviseeing you some time.

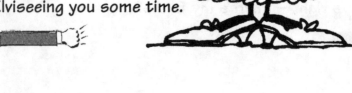

Knock knock.
Who's there?
Euripides.
Euripides who?
Euripides, you pay for a new pair.

Knock knock.
Who's there?
Farrah.
Farrah who?
Farrah 'nough.

Knock knock.
Who's there?
Fergie.
Fergie who?
Fergiedness sake let me in!

Knock knock.
Who's there?
Fonda.
Fonda who?
Fonda my family.

Knock knock.
Who's there?
Ford.
Ford who?
Ford he's a jolly good fellow.

Knock knock.
Who's there?
Frankenstein.
Frankenstein who?
Frankenstein his own name now.

Knock knock.
Who's there?
Frasier.
Frasier who?
Frasier going through.

Knock knock.
Who's there?
Friends.
Friends who?
Friends-ied attack.

Knock knock.
Who's there?
Gable.
Gable who?
Gable to leap tall buildings in a single bound.

Knock knock.
Who's there?
Gandhi.
Gandhi who?
Gandhi come out to play?

Knock knock.
Who's there?
Gaskill.
Gaskill who?
Gaskills if it's not turned off.

Knock knock.
Who's there?
Gazza.
Gazza who?
Gazza kiss.

Knock knock.
Who's there?
Grimm.
Grimm who?
Grimm and bear it.

Knock knock.
Who's there?
Handel.
Handel who?
Handel with care.

Knock knock.
Who's there?
Harlow.
Harlow who?
Harlow can you go?

Knock knock.
Who's there?
Haydn.
Haydn who?
Haydn the shed.

Knock knock.
Who's there?
Hepburn.
Hepburn who?
Hepburn and indigestion.

Knock knock.
Who's there?
Hobbit.
Hobbit who?
Hobbit-forming.

Knock knock.
Who's there?
Ivana.
Ivana who?
Ivana be rich.

Knock knock.
Who's there?
Jagger.
Jagger who?
Jaggered edge.

Knock knock.
Who's there?
Jaws.
Jaws who?
Jaws which one you want.

Knock knock.
Who's there?
Keanu.
Keanu who?
Keanu let me in? It's cold out here.

Knock knock.
Who's there?
Keats.
Keats who?
Keats you warm in the winter.

Knock knock.
Who's there?
Kermit.
Kermit who?
Kermit a crime and you go to jail.

Knock knock.
Who's there?
Khomeini.
Khomeini who?
Khomeini old time for dinner.

Knock knock.
Who's there?
Kylie.
Kylie who?
Kyliet your dog out for a walk?

Knock knock.
Who's there?
Lineker.
Lineker who?
Linekers in a big traffic jam.

Knock knock.
Who's there?
Liszt.
Liszt who?
Liszt of ingredients.

Knock knock.
Who's there?
Lulu.
Lulu who?
Lulu's not working, can I use yours?

Knock knock.
Who's there?
Lumley.
Lumley who?
Lumley cakes!

Knock knock.
Who's there?
Madonna.
Madonna who?
Madonna's being mean – tell her off!

Knock knock.
Who's there?
Mao.
Mao who?
Mao'th of babes.

Knock knock.
Who's there?
McEnroe.
McEnroe who?
McEnroe fast with his own oar.

Knock knock.
Who's there?
Metallica.
Metallica who?
Metallicand sleek looks are the best for cars.

Knock knock.
Who's there?
Miss Piggy.
Miss Piggy who?
Miss Piggy went to market,
Miss Piggy stayed at home ...

Knock knock.
Who's there?
Morrissey.
Morrissey who?
Morrissey the pretty birdies?

Knock knock.
Who's there?
Moses.
Moses who?
Moses the lawn.

Knock knock.
Who's there?
Mozart.
Mozart who?
Mozart is very beautiful.

Knock knock.
Who's there?
Mulder.
Mulder who?
Mulder on your old piece of cheese.

Knock knock.
Who's there?
Noah.
Noah who?
Noah counting for taste.

Knock knock.
Who's there?
Oasis.
Oasis who?
Oasis, let your brother in!

Knock knock.
Who's there?
Parton.
Parton who?
Parton my language.

Knock knock.
Who's there?
Pfeiffer.
Pfeiffer who?
Pfeiffer hours to Australia.

Knock knock.
Who's there?
Pulp.
Pulp who?
Pulp pretty hard on the door – it's stiff.

Knock knock.
Who's there?
The Queen.
The Queen who?
The Queen of the cwop.

Knock knock.
Who's there?
Reagan.
Reagan who?
Reagan maniac.

Knock knock.
Who's there?
Ringo.
Ringo who?
Ring of truth.

Knock knock.
Who's there?
Saddam.
Saddam who?
Saddam I that you couldn't come to the party.

Knock knock.
Who's there?
Schubert.
Schubert who?
Schubert I can.

Knock knock.
Who's there?
Scully.
Scully who?
Scully-wag!

Knock knock.
Who's there?
Sherlock.
Sherlock who?
Sherlock your door – someone could break in.

Knock knock.
Who's there?
Sheryl Crow.
Sheryl Crow who?
Sheryl Crow to the movies tonight?

Knock knock.
Who's there?
Sinatra.
Sinatra who?
Sinatra be a law.

Knock knock.
Who's there?
Sondheim.
Sondheim who?
Sondheim soon we'll meet again.

Knock knock.
Who's there?
Spillane.
Spillane who?
Spillane that knock knock joke!

Knock knock.
Who's there?
Spock.
Spock who?
Spocken like a true gentleman.

Knock knock.
Who's there?
Stalin.
Stalin who?
Stalin for time.

Knock knock.
Who's there?
Supergrass.
Supergrass who?
Supergrass on your lawn!

Knock knock.
Who's there?
Tarzan.
Tarzan who?
Tarzan stripes forever!

Knock knock.
Who's there?
Tolkein.
Tolkein who?
Tolkein for money off cornflakes.

Knock knock.
Who's there?
Truman.
Truman who?
Truman and honest men are needed for the jury.

Knock knock.
Who's there?
Tyson.
Tyson who?
Tyson of this for size.

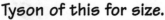

Knock knock.
Who's there?
UB40.
UB40 who?
UB40 today – happy birthday!

Knock knock.
Who's there?
Verdi.
Verdi who?
Verdia want to go?

Knock knock.
Who's there?
Vivaldi.
Vivaldi who?
Vivaldi books, there's nothing to read?

Knock knock.
Who's there?
Wedgwood.
Wedgwood who?
Wedgwood come if he could, but he's busy.

Knock knock.
Who's there?
Wet Wet Wet.
Wet Wet Wet who?
Wet Wet Wet out here – pass me an umbrella.

Knock knock.
Who's there?
Whoopi.
Whoopi who?
Whoopi cushion.

Chapter 4

Fantastic food

Knock knock.
Who's there?
Turnip.
Turnip who?
Turnip the stereo, I can't hear it.

Knock knock.
Who's there?
Apple.
Apple who?
Apple your hair if you don't let me in!

Knock knock.
Who's there?
Avocado.
Avocado who?
Avocado a cold!

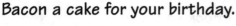

Knock knock.
Who's there?
Bacon.
Bacon who?
Bacon a cake for your birthday.

Knock knock.
Who's there?
Bean.
Bean who?
Bean fishing lately?

Knock knock.
Who's there?
Beets.
Beets who?
Beets me!

Knock knock.
Who's there?
Brie.
Brie who?
Brie me the head of John the Baptist!

Knock knock.
Who's there?
Butter.
Butter who?
Butter bring an umbrella – looks like rain.

Knock knock.
Who's there?
Carrot.
Carrot who?
Carrot me back to Old Virginia.

Knock knock.
Who's there?
Celery.
Celery who?
Celery me your lunch for 50p.

Knock knock.
Who's there?
Cherry.
Cherry who?
Cherry Lewis!

Knock knock.
Who's there?
Chicken.
Chicken who?
Chicken the oven – I think something's burning.

Knock knock.
Who's there?
Chow mein.
Chow mein who?
Chow mein to meet you, my dear.

Knock knock.
Who's there?
Curry.
Curry who?
Curry my bags, they're really heavy.

Knock knock.
Who's there?
Dill.
Dill who?
Dill we meet again.

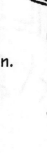

Knock knock.
Who's there?
Egg.
Egg who?
Egg-citing to meet you at last.

Knock knock.
Who's there?
Falafel.
Falafel who?
Falafel my bike and broke my arm.

Knock knock.
Who's there?
Figs.
Figs who?
Figs the doorbell, it's broken.

Knock knock.
Who's there?
Fruit.
Fruit who?
Fruit of the loom.

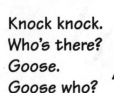

Knock knock.
Who's there?
Goose.
Goose who?
Goose see a doctor, you look sick.

Knock knock.
Who's there?
Grapes.
Grapes who?
Grapes Suzette.

Knock knock.
Who's there?
Gravy.
Gravy who?
Gravy Crockett.

Knock knock.
Who's there?
Halibut.
Halibut who?
Halibut a kiss, darling?

Knock knock.
Who's there?
Ice cream.
Ice cream who?
Ice cream of Jeannie.

Knock knock.
Who's there?
Ketchup.
Ketchup who?
Ketchup the tree again!

Knock knock.
Who's there?
Lemon.
Lemon who?
Lemon me give you a kiss.

Knock knock.
Who's there?
Lime.
Lime who?
Lime bean!

Knock knock.
Who's there?
Muffin.
Muffin who?
Muffin wrong with me – how about you?

Knock knock.
Who's there?
Okra.
Okra who?
Okra Winfrey.

Knock knock.
Who's there?
Olive.
Olive who?
Olive you.

Knock knock.
Who's there?
Omelette.
Omelette who?
Omelette'in you kiss me.

Knock knock.
Who's there?
Orange.
Orange who?
Orange you even going to open the door?

Knock knock.
Who's there?
Pasta.
Pasta who?
Pasta point of no return.

Knock knock.
Who's there?
Pears.
Pears who?
Pears the party?

Knock knock.
Who's there?
Peas.
Peas who?
Peas of the rock.

Knock knock.
Who's there?
Pecan.
Pecan who?
Pecan someone your own size.

Knock knock.
Who's there?
Pizza.
Pizza who?
Pizza the pie.

Knock knock.
Who's there?
Plums.
Plums who?
Plums me you'll always love me!

Knock knock.
Who's there?
Salmon.
Salmon who?
Salmonchanted evening.

Knock knock.
Who's there?
Sherbet.
Sherbet who?
Sherbet Forest!

Knock knock.
Who's there?
Soup.
Soup who?
Souperman!

Chapter 5

Paradise places

Knock knock.
Who's there?
Russia.
Russia who?
Russia little more if you want to get there on time.

Knock knock.
Who's there?
Alaska.
Alaska who?
Alaska one more time.

Knock knock.
Who's there?
Alberta.
Alberta who?
Alberta'll be over in a few minutes.

Knock knock.
Who's there?
Amazon.
Amazon who?
Amazon very bad mood.

Knock knock.
Who's there?
Ankara.
Ankara who?
Ankara went off the cliff.

Knock knock.
Who's there?
Ann.
Ann who?
Ann Tarctic.

Knock knock.
Who's there?
Arkansas.
Arkansas who?
Arkansas through any piece of wood.

Knock knock.
Who's there?
Asia.
Asia who?
Asia mother in?

Knock knock.
Who's there?
Athens.
Athens who?
Athens a dithturbance in the force.

Knock knock.
Who's there?
Austin.
Austin who?
Austin I forget things.

Knock knock.
Who's there?
Beirut.
Beirut who?
Beirut force.

Knock knock.
Who's there?
Belize.
Belize who?
Oh, Belize yourself then.

Knock knock.
Who's there?
Benin.
Benin who?
Benin any good shops lately?

Knock knock.
Who's there?
Berlin.
Berlin who?
Berlint me some books.

Knock knock.
Who's there?
Bolivia.
Bolivia who?
Bolivia me, I know what I'm talking about.

Knock knock.
Who's there?
Bologna.
Bologna who?
Bologna and cheese.

Knock knock.
Who's there?
Bosnia.
Bosnia who?
Bosnia bell here earlier?

Knock knock.
Who's there?
Brazil.
Brazil who?
Brazil hold your breasts up!

Knock knock.
Who's there?
Brighton.
Brighton who?
Brighton this side of the mountain.

Knock knock.
Who's there?
Chad.
Chad who?
Chad you could come.

Knock knock.
Who's there?
Chile.
Chile who?
Chile without your coat on!

Knock knock.
Who's there?
China.
China who?
China like old times, isn't it?

Knock knock.
Who's there?
Cologne.
Cologne who?
Cologne around the world and meet people.

Knock knock.
Who's there?
Congo.
Congo who?
Congo into town –
  it's dangerous.

Knock knock.
Who's there?
Crete.
Crete who?
Crete to see you.

Knock knock.
Who's there?
Cuba.
Cuba who?
Cuba wood.

Knock knock.
Who's there?
Cyprus.
Cyprus who?
Cyprus the bell?

Knock knock.
Who's there?
Czech.
Czech who?
Czech and see.

Knock knock.
Who's there?
Delhi.
Delhi who?
Delhi a joke ...

Knock knock.
Who's there?
Denmark.
Denmark who?
Denmark your own territory.

Knock knock.
Who's there?
Dublin.
Dublin who?
Dublin up with laughter.

Knock knock.
Who's there?
Egypt.
Egypt who?
Egypt me out in the cold!

Knock knock.
Who's there?
Essen.
Essen who?
Essen it fun hearing knock knock jokes?

Knock knock.
Who's there?
Europe.
Europe who?
Europening the door very slowly.

Knock knock.
Who's there?
Florida.
Florida who?
Florida room is sticky.

Knock knock.
Who's there?
France.
France who?
France of the family.

Knock knock.
Who's there?
Galway.
Galway who?
Galway you silly boy.

Knock knock.
Who's there?
Germany.
Germany who?
Germany people knock on your door?

Knock knock.
Who's there?
Ghana.
Ghana who?
Ghana get me a gun and go into town.

Knock knock.
Who's there?
Ghent.
Ghent who?
Ghent out of town.

Knock knock.
Who's there?
Giza.
Giza who?
Giza nice boy.

Knock knock.
Who's there?
Glasgow.
Glasgow who?
Glasgow to the movies.

Knock knock.
Who's there?
Gorky.
Gorky who?
Gorky will open the door.

Knock knock.
Who's there?
Greece.
Greece who?
Greece my palm and I'll tell you.

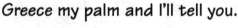

Knock knock.
Who's there?
Guinea.
Guinea who?
Guinea a high five!

Knock knock.
Who's there?
Haifa.
Haifa who?
Haifa pound is better than none.

Knock knock.
Who's there?
Haiti.
Haiti who?
Haitit when you get like that!

Knock knock.
Who's there?
Halifax.
Halifax who?
Halifax you, if you'll fax me.

Knock knock.
Who's there?
Havana.
Havana who?
Havana great time here!

Knock knock.
Who's there?
Hawaii.
Hawaii who?
Hawaii getting on?

Knock knock.
Who's there?
Holland.
Holland who?
Holland you going to make me wait?

Knock knock.
Who's there?
Idaho.
Idaho who?
Idaho'd the whole garden, but I was tired.

Knock knock.
Who's there?
India.
India who?
Indiafternoon I
  get sleepy.

Knock knock.
Who's there?
Indiana.
Indiana who?
Indiannals of history, you'll be famous.

Knock knock.
Who's there?
Iowa.
Iowa who?
Iowa lot to you.

Knock knock.
Who's there?
Iran.
Iran who?
Iran all the way home.

Knock knock.
Who's there?
Iraq.
Iraq who?
Iraq of lamb for dinner, please.

Knock knock.
Who's there?
Ireland.
Ireland who?
Ireland is the best land in the world.

Knock knock.
Who's there?
Italy.
Italy who?
Italy be a big job.

KNOCK!
KNOCK!

Knock knock.
Who's there?
Jamaica.
Jamaica who?
Jamaica mistake?

Knock knock.
Who's there?
Japan.
Japan who?
Japan is too hot – turn the hob down.

258

Knock knock.
Who's there?
Kansas.
Kansas who?
Kansas the best way to buy tuna.

Knock knock.
Who's there?
Kenya.
Kenya who?
Kenya guess?

Knock knock.
Who's there?
Kyoto.
Kyoto who?
Kyoto town tonight!

Knock knock.
Who's there?
Laos.
Laos who?
Laos and found.

Knock knock.
Who's there?
Leon.
Leon who?
Leonly one for me.

Knock knock.
Who's there?
Lisbon.
Lisbon who?
Lisbon away for a long time.

Knock knock.
Who's there?
Lodz.
Lodz who?
Lodz of fun.

Knock knock.
Who's there?
Lucerne.
Lucerne who?
Lucerne my trousers – I've eaten too much!

Knock knock.
Who's there?
Madrid.
Madrid who?
Madrid you wash my sports kit?

Knock knock.
Who's there?
Maine.
Maine who?
Maine reason I'm here!

Knock knock.
Who's there?
Mali.
Mali who?
Mali this at the post office.

Knock knock.
Who's there?
Manitoba.
Manitoba who?
Manitoba me hours to get there.

Knock knock.
Who's there?
Mecca.
Mecca who?
Mecca my day!

Knock knock.
Who's there?
Minsk.
Minsk who?
Minsk meat.

Knock knock.
Who's there?
Missouri.
Missouri who?
Missouri me!

Knock knock.
Who's there?
Montana.
Montana who?
Montana your hide if she finds out you broke her plate.

Knock knock.
Who's there?
Moscow.
Moscow who?
Moscow home soon.

Knock knock.
Who's there?
Munich.
Munich who?
Munich some money from me?

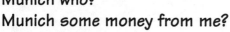

Knock knock.
Who's there?
Nebraska.
Nebraska who?
Nebraska girl for a date, she might say yes!

Knock knock.
Who's there?
Norway.
Norway who?
Norway is this your house – it's too grand!

Knock knock.
Who's there?
Odessa.
Odessa who?
Odessa good joke.

Knock knock.
Who's there?
Ohio.
Ohio who?
Ohio to you, too.

Knock knock.
Who's there?
Oman.
Oman who?
Oman, are you cute.

Knock knock.
Who's there?
Ottawa.
Ottawa who?
Ottawa to go to bed.

Knock knock.
Who's there?
Paris.
Paris who?
Paris the pepper, please.

Knock knock.
Who's there?
Perth.
Perth who?
Perth full of money.

Knock knock.
Who's there?
Peru.
Peru who?
Peruse this map before you go.

Knock knock.
Who's there?
Prussia.
Prussia who?
Prussia cooker.

Knock knock.
Who's there?
Quebec.
Quebec who?
Quebec to where you came from.

Knock knock.
Who's there?
Rio.
Rio who?
Riorrange your appointment please.

Knock knock.
Who's there?
Rome.
Rome who?
Romeing around.

Knock knock.
Who's there?
Russia.
Russia who?
Russia little more if you want to get there on time.

Knock knock.
Who's there?
Seoul.
Seoul who?
Seoul food.

Knock knock.
Who's there?
Seville.
Seville who?
Seville you play with me?

Knock knock.
Who's there?
Sienna.
Sienna who?
Siennathing good at the movies?

Knock knock.
Who's there?
Sofia.
Sofia who?
Sofia me, I'm hungry.

Knock knock.
Who's there?
Spain.
Spain who?
Spaint all over the wall.

Knock knock.
Who's there?
Sweden.
Sweden who?
Sweden the pill with some sugar.

Knock knock.
Who's there?
Taipei.
Taipei who?
Taipei 70 words a minute is fast.

Knock knock.
Who's there?
Tehran.
Tehran who?
Tehran and look me in the eye.

Knock knock.
Who's there?
Tennessee.
Tennessee who?
Tennessee is played at Wimbledon.

Knock knock.
Who's there?
Texas.
Texas who?
Texas are getting higher every year.

Knock knock.
Who's there?
Toronto.
Toronto who?
Toronto be a law against this.

Knock knock.
Who's there?
Tripoli.
Tripoli who?
Tripoli play.

Chapter 6

Cute couples

Knock knock.
Who's there?
Luke and Yul.
Luke and Yul who?
Luke through the keyhole and Yul see.

Knock knock.
Who's there?
Abbott and Costello.
Abbott and Costello who?
Abbott that Man United would win and now it'll
 Costello a lot of money.

Knock knock.
Who's there?
Ada and Ina.
Ada and Ina who?
Ada big dinner and Ina got sick.

Knock knock.
Who's there?
Adam and Eve.
Adam and Eve who?
Adam broke and Even the lake was flooded.

Knock knock.
Who's there?
Agate and Obsidian.
Agate and Obsidian who?
Agate your message and Obsidian here waiting for you.

Knock knock.
Who's there?
Al and Eda.
Al and Eda who?
Al and Eda love, love, Al and Eda love.

Knock knock.
Who's there?
Ali and Barbara.
Ali and Barbara who?
Ali Barbara and the Forty Thieves.

Knock knock.
Who's there?
Alva and Alma.
Alva and Alma who?
Alva day long Alma waiting
 for you to answer the door.

Knock knock.
Who's there?
Anatol and Hugh.
Anatol and Hugh who?
Anatol Hugh already who I am.

Knock knock.
Who's there?
Annie and Evie.
Annie and Evie who?
Anniebody and Eviebody.

Knock knock.
Who's there?
Asta and Attila.
Asta and Attila who?
Asta me no questions and Attila you no lies.

Knock knock.
Who's there?
Audrey and Rose.
Audrey and Rose who?
Audrey and Rose early in the morning.

Knock knock.
Who's there?
Avis and Hertz.
Avis and Hertz who?
Avis stung by a bee and it Hertz.

Knock knock.
Who's there?
Bea and Len.
Bea and Len who?
Bea friend and Len me some money.

Knock knock.
Who's there?
Beth and Connie.
Beth and Connie who?
Beth wishes and Conniegratulations.

Knock knock.
Who's there?
Betty and Lou.
Betty and Lou who?
Betty Lou all your money on the stock market.

Knock knock.
Who's there?
Brook and Lynn.
Brook and Lynn who?
Brooklyn, New York silly.

Knock knock.
Who's there?
Butch and Jimmie.
Butch and Jimmie who?
Butch your arms around me and Jimmie a kiss.

Knock knock.
Who's there?
Cain and Abel.
Cain and Abel who?
Cain play today – Abel to tomorrow.

Knock knock.
Who's there?
Canon and Rector.
Canon and Rector who?
Canon drive and Rector the car.

Knock knock.
Who's there?
Carmen and Cohen.
Carmen and Cohen who?
Carmen on Friday and
  Cohen on Sunday.

Knock knock.
Who's there?
Carrie and Clay.
Carrie and Clay who?
Carrie me home and Clay me down, I'm tired.

Knock knock.
Who's there?
Danielle and Butch.
Danielle and Butch who?
Danielle at me and Butch a smile on your face.

Knock knock.
Who's there?
Dude and Ron.
Dude and Ron who?
Duderonomy.

Knock knock.
Who's there?
Dutch and Hugh.
Dutch and Hugh who?
Dutch me and Hugh'll be sorry.

Knock knock.
Who's there?
Effie and Ida.
Effie and Ida who?
Effie'd known you were coming, Ida baked a cake.

Knock knock.
Who's there?
Eileen and Ringo.
Eileen and Ringo who?
Eileen against the door and Ringo the bell.

Knock knock.
Who's there?
Emily and Grace.
Emily and Grace who?
Emily Grace me, my sweet embraceable you.

Knock knock.
Who's there?
Esau and Evan.
Esau and Evan who?
Esau a ghost and Evan't
  been the same since.

Knock knock.
Who's there?
Evan and Ethan.
Evan and Ethan who?
Evan a barbeque and Ethan sausages.

Knock knock.
Who's there?
Eyes and Ears.
Eyes and Ears who?
Eyes got another knock knock joke and Ears it is.

Knock knock.
Who's there?
Fedora and Derby.
Fedora and Derby who?
Fedora's shut and Derby no one home.

Knock knock.
Who's there?
Fergie and Liza.
Fergie and Liza who?
Fergie Liza the lawn tomorrow.

Knock knock.
Who's there?
Frank and Bea.
Frank and Bea who?
Frank and Beans.

Knock knock.
Who's there?
Gunnar and Flo.
Gunnar and Flo who?
Gunnar huff and puff and Flo your house down.

Knock knock.
Who's there?
Halibut and Lemming.
Halibut and Lemming who?
Halibut opening this door and Lemming me in?

Knock knock.
Who's there?
Hobbit and Pixie.
Hobbit and Pixie who?
Hobbit letting me in and Pixie me some lunch?

Knock knock.
Who's there?
Hook and Dial.
Hook and Dial who?
Hook and Dial Dundee.

Knock knock.
Who's there?
Hope and Hugh.
Hope and Hugh who?
Hopen the door and Hugh'll see.

Knock knock.
Who's there?
Hugh and Alcott.
Hugh and Alcott who?
Hugh pour the tea and Alcott the cake.

Knock knock.
Who's there?
Ida and Bernie.
Ida and Bernie who?
Ida Bernie the toast.

Knock knock.
Who's there?
Igor and Ira.
Igor and Ira who?
Igor away and Ira-turn.

Knock knock.
Who's there?
Ike and Ali.
Ike and Ali who?
Ike kept knocking and
Ali time you knew it was me.

Knock knock.
Who's there?
Ike, Isa and Icon.
Ike, Isa and Icon who?
I came, I saw and I conquered.

Knock knock.
Who's there?
Ike and Tilly.
Ike and Tilly who?
Ike and Tilly phone you later.

Knock knock.
Who's there?
Ima and Howie.
Ima and Howie who?
Ima fine, and Howie you?

Knock knock.
Who's there?
Isa and Alma.
Isa and Alma who?
Isa you and Alma in love.

Knock knock.
Who's there?
Jess and Levy.
Jess and Levy who?
Jess go away and Levy me alone.

Knock knock.
Who's there?
Jim and Tom.
Jim and Tom who?
Jim and Tomic.

Knock knock.
Who's there?
Jimmy and Don.
Jimmy and Don who?
Jimmy my money and Don mess around.

Knock knock.
Who's there?
Jimmy and Hy.
Jimmy and Hy who?
Jimmy a pound and Hy'll pay you back.

Knock knock.
Who's there?
Jung and Freud.
Jung and Freud who?
Jung as a puppy and Freud of his own shadow.

Knock knock.
Who's there?
Keith and Cosmo.
Keith and Cosmo who?
Keith on complaining
 and you'll Cosmo trouble.

Knock knock.
Who's there?
Ken and Wayne.
Ken and Wayne who?
Ken I come in and wait for the Wayne to stop?

Knock knock.
Who's there?
Kermit and Althea.
Kermit and Althea who?
Kermit a crime and Althea in court.

Knock knock.
Who's there?
Largo and Andante.
Largo and Andante who?
Largo visit my uncle Andante.

Knock knock.
Who's there?
Leek and Hal.
Leek and Hal who?
Leek Hal weapon.

Knock knock.
Who's there?
Leslie and Lee.
Leslie and Lee who?
Leslie the party and Bea alone.

Knock knock.
Who's there?
Lettuce and Will.
Lettuce and Will who?
Lettuce in and Will stop bothering you.

Knock knock.
Who's there?
Lewis and Maude.
Lewis and Maude who?
Lewis all your money and Maude as well go home.

Knock knock.
Who's there?
Lucinda and Les.
Lucinda and Les who?
Lucinda chain
   and Les me in.

Knock knock.
Who's there?
Lucy and Desi.
Lucy and Desi who?
Lucy you belt and Desi a reason why your trousers
fall down.

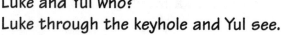

Knock knock.
Who's there?
Luke and Yul.
Luke and Yul who?
Luke through the keyhole and Yul see.

Knock knock.
Who's there?
Maia and Yvette.
Maia and Yvette who?
Maia cat was sick and Yvette made her better.

Knock knock.
Who's there?
Meg and Ada.
Meg and Ada who?
Meg a cake and Ada the whole thing.

Knock knock.
Who's there?
Meg and Cher.
Meg and Cher who?
Meg some cookies and Cher them with me.

Knock knock.
Who's there?
Meg and Lyle.
Meg and Lyle who?
Meg that shot and Lyle be a monkey's uncle.

Knock knock.
Who's there?
Megan and Chick.
Megan and Chick who?
Megan a list and Chick'in it twice.

Knock knock.
Who's there?
Mike and Angel.
Mike and Angel who?
Mike and Angelo's *David*.

Knock knock.
Who's there?
Muffin and Toby.
Muffin and Toby who?
Muffin to do but Toby lazy.

Knock knock.
Who's there?
Nanny and Ida.
Nanny and Ida who?
Nanny my friends any money and Ida either.

Knock knock.
Who's there?
Noble and Peer.
Noble and Peer who?
Noble, so I knocked, and Peer you are.

Knock knock.
Who's there?
O'Keefe and Hugh.
O'Keefe and Hugh who?
O'Keefe me one more chance and Hugh won't regret it.

Knock knock.
Who's there?
Olga and Greta.
Olga and Greta who?
Olga home and Greta my keys.

Knock knock.
Who's there?
Omega or Alpha.
Omega or Alpha who?
Omega your mind or Alpha go away.

Knock knock.
Who's there?
Oz and Toto.
Oz and Toto who?
Oz cold and Totolly frozen.

Knock knock.
Who's there?
Pappy and Bertha.
Pappy and Bertha who?
Pappy Berthaday.

Knock knock.
Who's there?
Pat and Lenny.
Pat and Lenny who?
Pat and Lenny shoes.

Knock knock.
Who's there?
Paul and Greta.
Paul and Greta who?
Paul cat's tail and you'll Greta scratch.

Knock knock.
Who's there?
Renata and Milt.
Renata and Milt who?
Renata Milt during the party.

Knock knock.
Who's there?
Rhoda and Will.
Rhoda and Will who?
Rhoda boat and Will
  get there faster.

Chapter 7

Hotch potch

Knock knock.
Who's there?
Handsome.
Handsome who?
Handsome dishes to me, I'll help wash.

Knock knock.
Who's there?
Armageddon.
Armageddon who?
Armageddon a new car.

Knock knock.
Who's there?
Avenue.
Avenue who?
Avenue learned my name yet?

Knock knock.
Who's there?
Atlas.
Atlas who?
Atlas report, England were winning.

Knock knock.
Who's there?
Baghdad.
Baghdad who?
Baghdad turkey.

Knock knock.
Who's there?
Bashful.
Bashful who?
Bashful of corn.

Knock knock.
Who's there?
Basket.
Basket who?
Basket in your glory.

Knock knock.
Who's there?
Bat.
Bat who?
Bat you can't wait to find out.

Knock knock.
Who's there?
Big Dipper.
Big Dipper who?
I Big to Dipper with you on that point.

Knock knock.
Who's there?
Bull.
Bull who?
Bull the chain.

Knock knock.
Who's there?
Bush.
Bush who?
Bush the door open.

Knock knock.
Who's there?
Canoe.
Canoe who?
Canoe let me in?

Knock knock.
Who's there?
Card.
Card who?
Card to please.

Knock knock.
Who's there?
Cargo.
Cargo who?
Cargo faster in fourth gear.

Knock knock.
Who's there?
Census.
Census who?
Census part of dollars.

Knock knock.
Who's there?
Chrome.
Chrome who?
Chromosome.

Knock knock.
Who's there?
Dachshund.
Dachshund who?
The ship will dachshund.

Knock knock.
Who's there?
Dawn.
Dawn who?
Dawn leave me out here alone.

Knock knock.
Who's there?
Denial.
Denial who?
Denial is a river in Egypt.

Knock knock.
Who's there?
Derby.
Derby who?
Derby only me here.

Knock knock.
Who's there?
Diesel.
Diesel who?
Diesel be the best jokes you ever heard.

Knock knock.
Who's there?
Diploma.
Diploma who?
Diploma to fix the leak.

Knock knock.
Who's there?
Disc.
Disc who?
Disc is my best joke.

Knock knock.
Who's there?
Dish.
Dish who?
Dish is shilly.

Knock knock.
Who's there?
Dismay.
Dismay who?
Dismay seem funny to you.

Knock knock.
Who's there?
Donatello.
Donatello who?
Donatello lie.

Knock knock.
Who's there?
Dopey.
Dopey who?
Dopey stupid.

Knock knock.
Who's there?
Fella.
Fella who?
Fella the leader.

Knock knock.
Who's there?
Frankenstein.
Frankenstein who?
Frankenstein the contract tomorrow.

Knock knock.
Who's there?
Gandhi.
Gandhi who?
Gandhi ropes.

Knock knock.
Who's there?
Golden Gate.
Golden Gate who?
Golden Gate me a cup of tea.

Knock knock.
Who's there?
Gnu.
Gnu who?
Gnu brooms sweep clean.

Knock knock.
Who's there?
Gorilla.
Gorilla who?
Gorilla me a steak.

Knock knock.
Who's there?
Gutter.
Gutter who?
Gutter some flowers and she'll forgive you.

Knock knock.
Who's there?
Hairy.
Hairy who?
Hairy up and open the door.

Knock knock.
Who's there?
Handsome.
Handsome who?
Handsome dishes to me, I'll help wash.

Knock knock.
Who's there?
Harmony.
Harmony who?
Harmony roads must
a man walk down?

Knock knock.
Who's there?
Haydn.
Haydn who?
Haydn out.

Knock knock.
Who's there?
Heifer.
Heifer who?
Heifer seen a ghost?

Knock knock.
Who's there?
Herd.
Herd who?
Herd my hand knocking on this door.

Knock knock.
Who's there?
Hose.
Hose who?
Hose been sleeping in my bed?

Knock knock.
Who's there?
Howl.
Howl who?
Howl in the world are you?

Knock knock.
Who's there?
Iguana.
Iguana who?
Iguana rule the world.

Knock knock.
Who's there?
Iowa.
Iowa who?
Iowa lot of money.

Knock knock.
Who's there?
Irene Dunne.
Irene Dunne who?
Irene Dunne a lot today.

Knock knock.
Who's there?
Ivory.
Ivory who?
Ivory about you.

Knock knock.
Who's there?
Jaws.
Jaws who?
Jaws truly.

Knock knock.
Who's there?
Jester.
Jester who?
Jester old-fashioned girl.

Knock knock.
Who's there?
Julie Andrews.
Julie Andrews who?
Julie Andrews a pretty picture.

Knock knock.
Who's there?
Kipper.
Kipper who?
Kipper the change.

Knock knock.
Who's there?
Kismet.
Kismet who?
Kismet, Hardy.

Knock knock.
Who's there?
Knees.
Knees who?
Kneester Bunny.

Knock knock.
Who's there?
Lasso.
Lasso who?
Lasso someone in the courts.

Knock knock.
Who's there?
Leaf.
Leaf who?
Leaf me alone.

Knock knock.
Who's there?
Lock.
Lock who?
Lock through the keyhole.

Knock knock.
Who's there?
Luke.
Luke who?
Luke out there's a monster behind you.

Knock knock.
Who's there?
Madonna.
Madonna who?
Madonna give me trouble.

Knock knock.
Who's there?
Malta.
Malta who?
Malta milk.

Knock knock.
Who's there?
Manchu.
Manchu who?
Manchu a lot.

Knock knock.
Who's there?
Miniature.
Miniature who?
Miniature open the door, you'll see.

Knock knock.
Who's there?
Mountain.
Mountain who?
Mountain of debts.

Knock knock.
Who's there?
Musket.
Musket who?
Musket a doorbell, I've been knocking for hours.

Knock knock.
Who's there?
Mustard.
Mustard who?
Mustard left my keys at work.

Knock knock.
Who's there?
Nanny.
Nanny who?
Nanny you mind.

Knock knock.
Who's there?
Ninja.
Ninja who?
Ninja just answer the door?

Knock knock.
Who's there?
Nike.
Nike who?
Nike night.

Knock knock.
Who's there?
Nobody.
Nobody who?
Nobody, get it?

Knock knock.
Who's there?
Oil.
Oil who?
Oil be seeing you.

Knock knock.
Who's there?
Paris.
Paris who?
Paris the broccoli please.

Knock knock.
Who's there?
Pasta.
Pasta who?
Pasta salt please.

Knock knock.
Who's there?
Pecan.
Pecan who?
Pecan boo.

Knock knock.
Who's there?
Perrot.
Perrot who?
Perrot away the rubbish.

Knock knock.
Who's there?
Phil.
Phil who?
Phil my face – is it getting furry?

Knock knock.
Who's there?
Phone.
Phone who?
Phonely me.

Knock knock.
Who's there?
Pencil.
Pencil who?
Pencil fall down if you forget your belt.

Knock knock.
Who's there?
Pill.
Pill who?
Pillowcase.

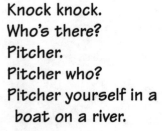

Knock knock.
Who's there?
Pitcher.
Pitcher who?
Pitcher yourself in a
  boat on a river.

Knock knock.
Who's there?
Pits.
Pits who?
Pits only a paper moon.

Knock knock.
Who's there?
Pizza.
Pizza who?
Pizza this, pizza that.

Knock knock.
Who's there?
Police.
Police who?
Police let me in.

Knock knock.
Who's there?
Radial.
Radial who?
Radial free Europe.

Knock knock.
Who's there?
Radio.
Radio who?
Radio not, here I come.

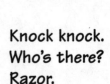

Knock knock.
Who's there?
Razor.
Razor who?
Razor hand if you have a question.

Knock knock.
Who's there?
Rio.
Rio who?
Riorrange your furniture.

Knock knock.
Who's there?
Rodin.
Rodin who?
Rodinto town on a horse.

Knock knock.
Who's there?
Santa Cruz.
Santa Cruz who?
Santa Cruz through the sky.

Knock knock.
Who's there?
Scold.
Scold who?
Scold at the South Pole.

Knock knock.
Who's there?
Sheik.
Sheik who?
Sheikspeare.

Knock knock.
Who's there?
Siena.
Siena who?
Siena good films recently?

Knock knock.
Who's there?
Sneezie.
Sneezie who?
Sneezie jolly good fellow.

Knock knock.
Who's there?
Snow.
Snow who?
Snow business of yours.

Knock knock.
Who's there?
Sofa.
Sofa who?
Sofa so good.

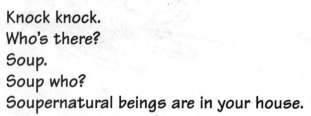

Knock knock.
Who's there?
Soup.
Soup who?
Soupernatural beings are in your house.

Knock knock.
Who's there?
Tango.
Tango who?
Tango away in the winter.

Knock knock.
Who's there?
Tennis.
Tennis who?
Tennis two times five.

Knock knock.
Who's there?
Toupee.
Toupee who?
Toupee is the first day of the rest of your life.

Knock knock.
Who's there?
Tooth.
Tooth who?
Tooth or dare.

Knock knock.
Who's there?
Toto.
Toto who?
Toto recall.

Knock knock.
Who's there?
Truman.
Truman who?
Truman are hard to find.

Knock knock.
Who's there?
Tuba.
Tuba who?
Tuba toothpaste.

Knock knock.
Who's there?
Vampire.
Vampire who?
Vampire State Building.

Knock knock.
Who's there?
Vaults.
Vaults who?
Vaultsing Matilda.

Knock knock.
Who's there?
Voodoo.
Voodoo who?
Voodoo you think you are?

Knock knock.
Who's there?
Wallet.
Wallet who?
Wallet it hurt you to open the door?

Knock knock.
Who's there?
Weasel.
Weasel who?
Weasel, you buy.

Knock knock.
Who's there?
Weevil.
Weevil who?
Weevil overcome.

Knock knock.
Who's there?
Yeast.
Yeast who?
Yeast is east and west is west.